WATER RESOURCES, GEOGRAPHY AND LAW

Olen Paul Matthews
Department of Geography
University of Idaho

RESOURCE PUBLICATIONS
IN GEOGRAPHY

P9-BJA-404

Library of Congress Card Number 84-70006
ISBN 0-89291-174-3

Library of Congress Cataloging in Publication Data

Matthews, Olen Paul, 1942-
    Water resources, geography and law.

    Bibliography: p.
    1. Water — Law and legislation — United States.   KF
2. Water-rights — United States. I. Title.   5569
KF5569.M34   1984   346.7304'691   84-70006   .M34
ISBN 0-89291-174-3   347.3064691   1984

Publication Supported by the A.A.G.

Graphic Design by CGK

Printed by Commercial Printing Inc.
State College, Pennsylvania

Foreword

That water is among the most fundamental and important resources to humanity is both obvious and profound. Water is simply indispensable in the biological and economic life of mankind. Water is equally central in the functioning of the biosphere — its quantity, its biological role, its thermal attributes, and its role in the planetary energy balance all suggest this centrality.

At one time it was possible to believe that water scarcity was a significant problem, economic handicap, or locational factor *only* in arid lands where water deficits prevailed. Such a view suggested that by looking to water-deficient areas, we could learn much about natural and societal processes in channelling water for productive use. This viewpoint ignored a reality that was to emerge: water supply problems in humid lands.

Water's role as a natural hazard was, of course, recognized, including floods and water-borne infection. However, the high population densities of urban areas, as well as the water demands of an industrial society, brought scarcity, sometimes drought, to seemingly well-watered areas. On a more local scale, individual landowners even in humid areas had been concerned about public and private water supply.

These regional and local, public and private, arid and humid land issues are addressed in Western legal traditions extending from the Roman era. Geographers have paid too little attention to law as a guiding element in many facets of natural resource use and landscape evolution, a fact particularly true with respect to water. In this book, Paul Matthews, geographer *and* attorney, demonstrates how the law interacts with natural and cultural processes related to water resources. Thus, this book serves two purposes. First, it adds to a small but growing body of literature linking geography and law as fundamental disciplines. Second, and perhaps most important, it demonstrates how attention to legal dimensions can enhance our continuing interest in water as a resource.

The *Resource Publications in Geography* are sponsored by the Association of American Geographers, a professional organization whose purpose is to advance studies in geography and to encourage application of geographic research in education, government, and business. Tracing its origins to the AAG's *Resource Papers* (1968-1974), the *Resource Publications* continue a tradition of presenting geographers' views on timely public and professional issues to colleagues, students, and fellow citizens. Views expressed, of course, are the author's and do not imply AAG endorsement.

The editor and advisory board commend *Water Resources, Geography and Law* to you. You will be intrigued by an attorney's perspective on familiar themes in geography and, hopefully, will be challenged to trace important legal dimensions of geographical themes beyond those discussed here.

C. Gregory Knight, *The Pennsylvania State University*
Editor, Resource Publications in Geography

Resource Publications Advisory Board

George W. Carey, *Rutgers University*
James S. Gardner, *University of Waterloo*
Charles M. Good, Jr., *Virginia Polytechnic Institute and State University*
Risa I. Palm, *University of Colorado*
Thomas J. Wilbanks, *Oak Ridge National Laboratory*

Preface

Water is one of the most important resources required for human survival. As a result, policies governing the use of water are critical. Today, water policies are being re-examined in the light of regional water shortages and water quality problems. Increased demands for water-oriented recreation and concern over water as wildlife habitat are creating conflicts with traditional uses. Current policies are not always adequate to resolve these problems and sometimes cause additional conflict. Since future water needs will increase the possibilities of conflict, the evaluation of current uses and policies needs to be accelerated.

In order to evaluate the impact of water policy and water use, there is a need to understand how law — the formalization of policy — relates to resource use. An understanding is needed also of the current law and how it developed. This book describes the law/resource connection and summarizes water law in three areas of geographical interest — public use, allocation of rights, and boundary changes.

The first area was chosen because the public's right to use rivers and lakes for recreation and other purposes reflects a change in the way property rights are perceived. Although there has always been a right to use the nation's water for commercial navigation, water not capable of this was considered private property. Increased demand is changing this distinction between public and private waters with the public's rights being expanded. The same trend is occurring with other property interests.

In the second area — water rights — the systems that evolved to control the allocation of rights to water are not necessarily suited for today's urbanized, industrialized society. The transfer of water out of a watershed may be prohibited, or changes from traditional places of use may be restricted. Conflicts exist between different government levels over who controls the allocation of these rights. Substantial reform may be needed if an equitable distribution of water is to be obtained in the future.

The third subject area — boundary changes — was chosen because it has a long history in the geographic literature and will continue to cause legal problems in the future. Recent court cases demonstrate the continuing nature of this legal issue.

Many other areas could have been chosen such as the laws related to ground water and water quality, but space was limited. Even the subjects covered are abbreviated. As a result, readers should be wary of generalizations about the law which may be misleading if used on a specific fact situation. Law is not bipolar but a continuum creating a variety of interpretations and codifications.

Special thanks go to Kathryn Toffenetti, an attorney and fellow in the Institute for Resource Management. Also, thank you to Sheldon Bluestein and the cartographers — Brian Raber and Meg Van Dyke.

Olen Paul Matthews

Contents

List of Figures

1

The Nature of Water and Its Use

On July 3, 1976, several people crossed public land to enter the Colorado River for a float trip. Their rafts were designed to draw five or six inches of water, and the minimum depth of the river in the area was twelve inches. Part of their river route was through private land where ownership of the river bed was claimed by a rancher. When the rancher learned of the rafters' approach, he strung barbed wire across the river eight to ten inches over its surface. He claimed they were trespassing because he owned the river bed. The rafters disagreed, claiming they had rights to float the river. The immediate dispute was resolved by a deputy sheriff who arrested several of the rafters on criminal trespass charges.

The rafters felt they had a right to be on the river because Colorado's constitution (Article XVI, Section 5) states that the water of natural streams is the property of the public. If the public owns the water, how could they be trespassing on it? The Colorado Supreme Court *(People v. Emmert* 1979) upheld the trespass conviction using a legal principle dating back to feudal England — *cujens est solum, ejus est usque ad coelum* — he who owns the surface of the ground has the exclusive right to everything above it. The opinion was not unanimous, however. In fact, the one dissenting judge chided the others, pointing out that the United States Supreme Court *(United States v. Causby* 1946) had abandoned this obsolete, antiquarian doctrine as having no place in the modern world. How could the Colorado Supreme Court uphold it?

There is a fifty mile stretch of the Mulberry River in Arkansas that can be floated six months of the year. Part of the river flows through private land. In 1975 six hundred members of a conservationist group put into the river at a public bridge near the McIlroy farm and floated through it. Mr. McIlroy tried to stop what he considered to be trespassing by bringing a law suit against the group and two canoe rental companies. The Arkansas Supreme Court *(State v. McIlroy* 1980) held that rivers capable of being used by recreationists were public rivers and private landowners cannot prohibit their use. This was based on the concept of 'navigability.' How is this case different from the one in Colorado? Should the results be the same when similar issues are raised?

An 1854 treaty with the Omaha Indians established a reservation on the western side of the Missouri River with the center of the river's channel being one boundary. A survey of part of the reservation was conducted in 1867, but since then the river has changed course, so that today much of the surveyed land is on the Iowa side of the river. Claiming this area had been settled illegally by non-Indians, the Bureau of Indian

Affairs and the tribe sought to gain possession of it in 1975. The battle over Blackbird Bend has been fought in the courts with the tribe winning most battles *(Wilson v. Omaha Indian Tribe* 1979). What happens to property rights when rivers change course? Does a landowner have a property right in every particle of soil no matter where it goes? If he loses land to a river, does he gain a right in land made by the river?

Several early treaties used the Mississippi River as a boundary. The location was the middle of the river or, as stated in the Louisiana Purchase, the middle of the main channel. However, between 1823 and 1876 a section dividing Arkansas and Tennessee was widened a half mile through natural processes. On March 7 and 8, 1876, the river made an entirely new channel, leaving part of Tennessee on the "wrong" side of the river. These events precipitated a dispute between Tennessee and Arkansas over the location of their boundary *(Arkansas v. Tennessee* 1918). Did the boundary change when the river changed course? Does the middle of the main channel mean an equal distance from each bank, or is it the middle of the channel of navigation? Since channel conditions change over time, which year should be used in establishing the boundary?

Adamson Draw in Wyoming drains about three hundred acres of land, most of which was owned by Mr. Hiber. A neighbor whose land was below Adamson Draw applied to the state for a permit to build a dam to catch runoff from rain and melting snow. While this dam was being constructed, Mr. Hiber built a separate one on his own property. Since he had no permit and his dam prevented runoff from reaching the approved one, the state went to court.

The area where Hiber's dam was built was dry except in the spring. It was coverd with grass, had no stream banks, and could be crossed almost everywhere in a vehicle. Hiber said the water was his and a state permit was not required. The Wyoming Supreme Court agreed *(State v. Hiber* 1935). How can a court do this if the water in a state belongs to the people? In Oklahoma an entire watershed owned by one party was dammed. The Oklahoma Supreme Court *(Oklahoma Water Resources Board v. Central Oklahoma Master Conservancy District* 1969) said existing rights granted by the state to others in the watershed were still valid, and the landowner could not capture them with his dam. How is this different from the Wyoming case?

In 1949 the Federal Power Commission (FPC) found there was a public need for a dam on the Deschutes River in Oregon. The state of Oregon challenged the authority of the FPC to issue the permit and questioned whether provisions for the preservation of anadromous fish were adequate. The dam was to built on federal land, and the United States Supreme Court held the state had no control over federal property *(Federal Power Commission v. Oregon* 1955).

In a similar situation the FPC issued a license to the City of Tacoma, Washington, to build a dam on the Cowlitz River. This time no federal property was involved; nevertheless the United States Supreme Court ruled *(City of Tacoma v. Taxpayers of Tacoma 1958)* against a citizens' group and the state of Washington who had tried to stop the dam. The court reasoned that the river was navigable and therefore subject to federal control under the commerce clause of the United States Constitution (Art. I, section 7, clause 3). How much control does the federal government have over the nation's water? Are water rights issued by states valid? Which level of government should control the allocation of water rights?

These are examples of the legal questions that have arisen over water management. Courts, legislative bodies, and administrative agencies at federal, state, and local levels are interested in the allocation of water rights and the way water is used. The reason for this is the supreme value placed on water by humankind. Even more than forming the basis for much of our social order, it sustains life itself. Such importance inevitably leads to conflicts over the rights to its use. Many such conflicts relate to water's mobility — anything that interferes with this movement may deprive someone of water they are accustomed to receiving. The hydrologic cycle explains the movement of water, and law has been developed to control the use of water in each part of the cycle.

The Hydrologic Cycle and the Law

Typical approaches to the hydrologic cycle focus on the processes by which water changes form and moves. These processes include precipitation, evaporation, transpiration, horizontal advection, overland flow, infiltration, percolation and condensation. Related is the unequal distribution of water over the earth's surface. The law treats each part of the hydrologic cycle in different ways (Templar 1973). The magnitude of this treatment depends upon the extent to which humans can influence the particular elements of the cycle (Figure 1). Atmospheric moisture, for example, is hard to control or capture. As a result, the laws concerning it are few and inconsistent. Surface water on the other hand, especially freshwater, can be more easily controlled. Thus, conflicts between users have been frequent, and as a result an extensive body of relevant law has developed. The more recent increasing use of subsurface water, meanwhile, has required a concurrent increase in the development of law in this area. Moreover, subsurface water's special characteristics have spawned a different set of legal problems than its surficial counterpart.

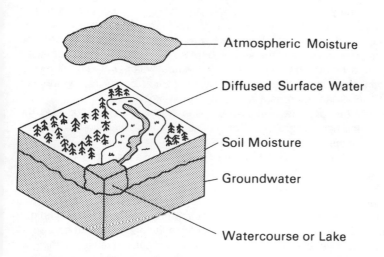

Atmospheric Moisture

Diffused Surface Water

Soil Moisture

Groundwater

Watercourse or Lake

FIGURE 1   THE HYDROLOGIC CYCLE AND ITS LEGAL
TERMINOLOGY

There is no way an extensive review of all water law can be accomplished in a short book. Nor is there room here for an extensive review of the literature on the hydrologic cycle. Chorley (1969) provides an excellent source on the hydrologic cycle as well as the interface between man and water. The remainder of this chapter attempts to explore the elemental links between law and the basic components of the hydrologic cycle.

Atmospheric Water

Until weather modification began there was no need for any law related to atmospheric water. Natural processes determined when and where precipitation would occur. Rain dances, mystics, and charlatans aside, it is only recently that the technology for weather modification has been developed (Dennis 1980; Wegman and De-Priest 1980). In 1946, for example, it was discovered that ice crystals form when dry ice comes in contact with super-cooled water droplets. This discovery eventually led to the use of propane and silver iodide to suppress hail and severe storms, disperse fog, and increase precipitation.

Once the technology developed the legal issues appeared (R.J. Davis 1984, 1978; Davis and Grant 1978). Who owns water in the atmosphere? Who owns the new water that is created? If someone is deprived of water they would otherwise have gotten, who is responsible? If increased rainfall causes property damage, who should pay? Are controls needed over who should modify weather, and under what circumstances? Do we know enough about weather modification to make adequate laws?

Until recently there were no statutes controlling the rights to atmospheric water, and the few existing court decisions came to different conclusions. In *Slutsky v. City of New York* (1950), a New York Court held landowners have no right to the clouds and atmospheric moisture over their land. A Texas case (*Southwest Weather Research v. Duncan* 1958) recognized a landowner's right to the rainfall that nature provides. In Pennsylvania landowners were held to have a property right in water over their land (*Pennsylvania Natural Weather Association v. Blue Ridge Weather Modification Association* 1968). In all three cases landowners were trying to stop cloud seeding efforts. Ownership of the moisture in the atmosphere above their land would prohibit a weather modifier from interfering with it. Obviously, without weather modification such ownership is not a legal issue, because the water cannot come into a person's possession until after it has fallen as a result of natural processes.

If the amount of rain or snow in a watershed is artificially increased, does the person who creates this have a right to it? Can the increase in precipitation be proved? If it can, how much of this increase reaches a stream?

Determining the amount of water added to a stream as a result of weather modification is a difficult problem to solve. Although scientists may be able to show there is an increase in precipitation, they also have to convince a judge or water administrator of the amount of increase. The time of seeding, cloud conditions where the seeding occurred, the intensity and duration of the precipitation, and the technique used are variables that must be considered. Hydrologic factors such as topography, soil conditions, ground cover and snow melt rate are also of consequence, as they will determine how much of the increased precipitation reaches a stream and is transported to the place of use.

Even when the amount of increase can be identified, states are inconsistent in granting rights to it. In Colorado the prior appropriation doctrine is used (Colo. Rev. Stat. Ann. § 36-20-101, 1973). In Utah it is considered part of the state's "basic water supply" (Utah Code Ann. § 73-15-4, 1978), and in North Dakota it is treated like "natural precipitation" (N.D. Cent. Code § 2-07-01, 1975). In appropriation states, increases in stream flow belong to the person who creates the increase in some instances. It is not clear from these statutes whether this would be true for increases in precipitation. These statutes do not mean the same thing.

Another major legal issue is determining responsibility for damages that occur because the hydrologic cycle has been interrupted (Fischer 1976; Pierce 1967). Damages can be in two forms — too much rain or too little. The 1977 drought in the Pacific Northwest was combated in Washington State by cloud seeding. The state of Idaho objected vigorously, claiming that Washington was stealing water that would have fallen on Idaho's mountains if the cloud seeding had not occurred. Rain, not the courts, resolved this issue. In general, there is no question that cloud seeding may cause harm to individuals from deprivation or excesses of moisture. The problem is proving that modification activities actually cause the harm. Would the harm have occurred "but for" the modification activities? Expert witnesses must be relied upon in making this determination, and they may rally around one of their own (Davis 1978b).

The law relating to atmospheric moisture is new and inconsistent. It is likely to remain so unless weather modification attempts increase in number or become more reliable. Although the majority of the states have some pertinent laws, most are related to the activities of the weather modifier. Typically, the state requires the individual to be licensed or hold a permit. In half the states modifiers must keep records and make reports (Farhar and Mews 1977). At the federal level the National Weather Modification Policy Act of 1976 (15 U.S.C. § 330, 1983 supp.) requires that weather modifiers report their activities.

Once atmospheric water falls, infiltrates through the soil, and becomes ground water, it is easier to control and put to a planned use. As a result the law relating to the allocation of ground water is well developed.

Ground Water

"Ground water is the water that penetrates the soil and reaches the water table" (Botkin and Keller 1982). Ground water may emerge from a spring after a short time beneath the surface, or it may remain locked up until wells are drilled and it is pumped to the surface. Subsurface water in the soil above the water table is generally treated by law as part of the soil. Plants can use it, but it cannot be pumped from a well. As a result most of the legal decisions related to subsurface water management concern only ground water. In the past, misinformation and mysticism plagued ground water, making it a province of quacks and pseudoscientists. They described unknown and unknowable movements of great rivers beneath the surface. Today divining rods are not needed, and although they may still be used, a scientific approach to ground water exists (Freeze and Cherry 1979; Todd 1980).

Because ground water moves, adjacent surface owners may be competing for the same water. If one well is deeper, it may cause a nearby one to go dry or require an increase in pumping lift. Over the years, four common law doctrines have evolved to control the allocation of ground water (Corker 1971). The "English rule" grants absolute ownership to all water below the surface to the surface owners. They have a right to anything they can pump. This is the law adhered to in Texas *(City of Corpus Christi v. City of Pleasanton* 1955). The results are similar in Louisiana where ground water is not owned until it is "captured and reduced to possession" *(Adams v. Grigsby* 1963).

In other states the "American rule" of reasonable use is followed. Each landowner is restricted to a reasonable exercise of his own rights and a reasonable use of his own property in view of the similar rights of others.

A third doctrine, the law of prior appropriation, prevails in many states, giving the person who first uses ground water a priority right over those subsequently desiring the same water. This is found in many western states where similar laws are used for surface water.

In California, meanwhile, the doctrine of correlative rights is enforced, requiring reasonable use with some notion of sharing between overlying landowners. In addition to this, priority rights control appropriators who remove the water from the overlying land.

Figure 2 classifies ground water law. From the four original systems developed at common law, a variety of permit systems has evolved. Except for the appropriation system, priority based on ownership of land overlying an aquifer is a common trait — the overlying rights theories. The appropriation doctrine is dominant in the West where it has replaced the older English doctrine (Aiken 1980).

In the East, permits are a relatively new development. Many of these states considered the appropriation system but rejected it (Mississippi has it for surface water). Very few have comprehensive regulatory systems. Exemptions from permits are common, as in Georgia where no permit is required for irrigation wells. In other states, only specified areas are covered (Ausness 1983). Nebraska, California and Texas have been classified as retaining one of the common law rights theories giving priority to the overlying land owner, even though a permit may be possible. In all three states complex systems have evolved with elements of local control (Johnson 1980).

There are several other problems associated with ground water use that have been addressed by the legal system. A percentage of ground water has to be looked on as stored water, because it is not now part of the hydrologic cycle. Surface waters never reach it, and it never reaches the surface by natural processes. If this water is used, it will be depleted and eventually exhausted. However, if it is not or cannot be used, it has no value and should not be considered a resource.

In other places ground water may be replenished from the surface, but if it is used faster than it is recharged, the ground water table will be lowered. Such use is called 'mining' and can lead to the exhaustion of an aquifer. States have reacted to this problem in different ways (Bagley 1961; National Water Commission 1973). South Dakota (So. Dak. Comp. L. § 46-6-3.1, 1983) and Idaho (I.C. § 42-237a(g), 1977; *Baker v. Ore-Ida Foods, Inc.* 1973) have statutes prohibiting withdrawals that exceed the natural recharge. In Oregon (Or. Rev. Stat. § § 537.730 & 537.735, 1981) and Wyoming (Wyo. Stat. § 41-3-912, 1977) areas may be closed to new wells and permits refused if state water officials declare the existence of a "critical area." In others the rate of depletion is controlled *(Mathers v. Texaco* 1966; *Fundingsland v. Colorado Ground Water Commission* 1970; National Water Commission 1973; Corker 1971).

Another kind of problem exists when there is a connection between ground water and surface water. If ground water is tributary to a stream, extracting it will reduce the amount of water that reaches the stream. If all the water in the stream is claimed by prior users then their rights may be harmed. Some states treat streams and tributary ground

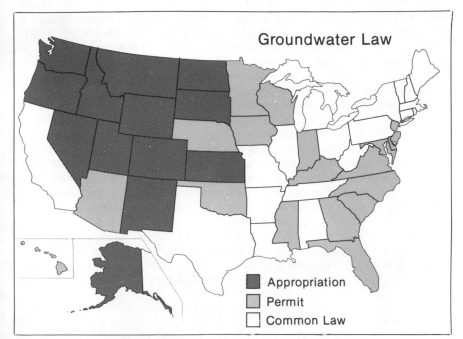

FIGURE 2   CLASSIFICATION OF STATE GROUND WATER
LAW (Aiken 1980; Ausness 1977, 1983; Clark 1977;
Grant 1981; Johnson 1980; Putt 1981)

water as a single management system *(Safranek v. Limon* 1951; *Hall v. Kuiper* 1973; Colo. Rev. Stat. § 37-92-101, 1982 supp.; *Albuquerque v. Reynolds* 1962; Wyo. Stat. § 41-3-911, 1977). In others the land owner may be allowed to take what he wants because he owns the water beneath his land *(Pecos County Water Control and Improvement Dist. v. Williams* 1954). Harrison and Sandstrom (1971) have written an excellent article which describes the conflicts that can occur between ground and surface water users and examines Colorado's legislative solution.

River Regimes and Variability

Precipitation does not occur in the same amounts at all places on the earth nor does it fall evenly throughout the year. As a result, there may be floods, droughts, or a need for irrigation. If there is not enough natural water for agricultural development, it can be stored in reservoirs until it is needed. The Reclamation Act of 1902 (434 U.S.C. § § 371-615, 1964), the Carey Act of 1894 (43 U.S.C. § 641, 1964) and the Reclamation Project Act of 1939 (43 U.S.C. § 485, 1964) are examples of federal legislation designed to encourage the development of arid lands through irrigation. At a different scale, local irrigation projects may be implemented by individuals or groups. If so, state and federal permits may be needed (Federal Power Act 16 U.S.C, § 701, 1974).

The federal government has long been interested in flood control. In 1936 a law (33 U.S.C. § 701, 1970) was passed which made it a national policy to have a continuing flood control program. The federal government has made flood insurance available under the National Flood Insurance Act of 1954 and 1968 (42 U.S.C. § 4011, 1977). The act requires state and local governments to pass land use control measures in these areas in order to reduce future damage. At the local level, as a result, flood plain zoning is common. Zoning does not prevent flooding, but it attempts to limit the amount of damage that will be done when floods occur (Plater 1974).

In water shortage areas it is not always possible to "store" water in a reservoir. At the same time ground water supplies may be inadequate. When this occurs plans may be made for importing water (Loeffler 1970; Quinn 1968). California residents want the Columbia River, and those on the South Plains eye the Missouri. Many states claim ownership of the water within their boundaries. This justifies statutes that would prohibit out-of-state water transfers. But in *Sporhase v. Nebraska* (1982), the United States Supreme Court held that water was an article of commerce. This means that many restrictions on water transfers may no longer exist. This will be discussed later under federal/state powers to control water allocation.

The location of water in the hydrologic cycle and differences in using and controlling it have created a complex set of laws. No where is this more true than with surface waters. For this reason the nature of rivers and lakes will be looked at in more detail, making this area of the hydrologic cycle our main topic.

Surface Water

The nature and properties of surface water influence the laws that have developed to regulate its use. In its natural form surface water comes into being when precipitation hits the ground. It may evaporate, or it may infiltrate, becoming subsurface water. Some of it may flow overland to a river or lake and eventually reach the ocean. Water that moves has energy, is capable of transporting soil particles and boulders, and is capable of weathering rock materials. Together these make water one of the principal agents involved in shaping the earth (Chorley 1969).

Between the time water hits the surface and reaches a river or lake, it is commonly called overland flow. Rain splash and sheetwash move particles downslope eroding rills and gullies. The movement downslope may be slight or it may contribute significant sediment to rivers and lakes. The function of water in this part of the hydrologic cycle was one reason Congress created the Soil Conservation Service (16 U.S.C. § 590e, 1974). Preventing soil erosion by advising on farm practices is just one of its roles. Studies have been funded and grants to farmers are available in some circumstances. Other federal laws such as the National Environmental Policy Act (42 U.S.C. § 4321, 1977) look at erosion along with other consequences of overland flow.

Once water reaches an open channel there are more legal controls over it because there are more competing uses. As a geomorphic agent, water in open channels may carry a great deal of sediment. Some of this sediment may be deposited along the banks of the river, or additional material can be taken from there. Erosion and deposition operate to modify the river, creating problems of land ownership and jurisdictional control. These have significant legal and geographic consequences.

Water in an open channel is ecologically significant, and some laws reflect this. The plants and animals living in a stream may be protected by law because they are endangered species. Even if they are not, the water quality may be controlled under the

Clean Water Act. The quality of the water and the protection of the species in it are legal approaches taken to maintain the ecology of rivers and lakes. Taking animals from a river may be regulated by requiring a license or closing a stream to fishing. Also, access to the stream may be limited by the legal system.

Besides being geomorphic and ecological agents, rivers flow and can be floated. The flow of rivers may be important for navigation and can be converted to energy. Because things float on water, logs are shipped to sawmills, barges take ore to smelters, grain is transported, and people use it for recreation.

Besides these instream uses there are those demands for which water is taken from the river. Irrigation, domestic uses, and industrial processes use water that is removed from the natural hydrologic cycle. In one sense, water that does not return to the stream is consumed because it is no longer available for other in-stream uses. Out-of-stream water uses may change the properties of a river so that the rates of erosion and deposition are different. Animals may no longer be able to survive if minimum stream flows required for their continued existence are not maintained. Consumption of water may reduce the potential for commercial and recreational river floating as well as reduce potential power generation. Consumption conflicts with the natural processes of the river and human in-stream uses. These uses compete with each other when insufficient water is available for all potential users, or when one use precludes another. As a result, a substantial body of law has developed to control the allocation of water rights. Conflicts exist between the state, federal, and private sectors regarding who controls the allocation process.

Before the laws controlling the use of rivers and lakes can be discussed, however, an understanding of the United States legal system is necessary.

2

Law and Resource Use

Law is an important variable in understanding and explaining the distributional patterns and spatial relationships associated with the use of water resources. The Clean Water Act, the National Enviromental Policy Act, and state water laws have a direct influence on how water resources are used. Other laws do also; sometimes they reflect contradictory policies at the local, state, or federal levels. Because of this, an understanding of the legal system is essential in understanding the way water resources are used. To clarify the relationship between law, society, and resource use, a model has been developed (Figure 3).

The relationship between law and geography has been explored by many authors. Whittlesey (1935, 1939) long ago recognized the impact of the law on the landscape. Today there is a general recognition of the relationship between law and resource management (Fielding 1965; Fitzsimmons 1980; Greenland 1983; Mitchell 1976, 1979). The impact laws have on the location of economic activities, the allocation of resources, and changes in the landscape are matters with which geographers must be concerned.

The Model

There are five principal elements in the model: (1) individual and societal goals; (2) process and structure; (3) legal/political action; (4) formal jurisdiction; and (5) resource field. These elements do not operate alone but are influenced by the bio-physical environment and the behavior of individuals within the system. Also, nonpolitical factors which influence resource use, such as the least cost principle, must be considered in any explanation.

There are several concepts or models in political geography that recognize the legal system as a geographic variable. Whittlesey's law-landscape approach has already been mentioned. Of equal significance to this study is the unified field theory created by Jones (1954) and tested by deBlij and Capone (1969). Jones built upon the ideas of Gottman (1952) and Hartshorne (1950) which concerned the formation and interrelationships of nation-states. The model discussed here is more limited in scope since it deals with water resources only. However, it could be used for other resources. For our discussion, resource "use" incorporates the concept of preservation as well as consumption.

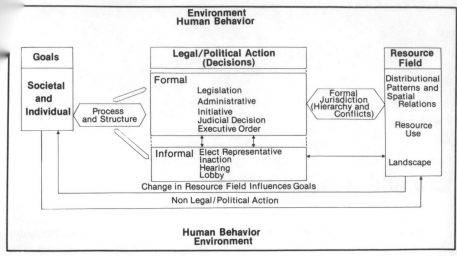

FIGURE 3   RESOURCE LEGAL MODEL

Legal systems are not the same all over the world, as was pointed out by Easterly (1977). The differences limit the use of the model to similar systems. It is also limited to a single country at a time, as most resource mangement and land use planning studies have been in the past (Ackerman *et.al.* 1965). For this reason, the approaches of Gottman and Hartshorne are not as useful as that of Jones, whose idea-area chain can be applied to the internal political functions of a country.

Another major influence in developing the model was Cohen and Rosenthal's (1971) geographic model for political systems analysis. This expands upon the works cited above and upon the systems theory used by Easton (1953, 1965). Although it has been said that "heuristic devices consisting of boxes and arrows seem less exciting than when first discovered," they "provide useful ways of organizing ideas" (Burnett and Taylor 1981). Even if the model presented here goes no further, an organizational tool is necessary to understand the legal system.

Platt's work (1976) which concentrated on land use control at the local level has also been useful because of its emphasis on the legal element. The same is true for Templar's work (1973), which related law to the hydrologic cycle.

Resource management and land use planning were recognized as a major problem area in political geography by Ackerman *et al.* (1965). Kasperson and Minghi (1969) recognized the need for political geography research in environmental problems. Recently Minghi has said this area of research had not blossomed as expected (Minghi 1981). Water resources are part of this research need. The model is an attempt to create, as Jones (1954) said, "a compact description, a clue to explanation, and a tool for better work" so that an understanding of water resources can be obtained.

Goals

The box marked "Goals" in Figure 3 represents the cultural, economic and psychological forces that determine societal and individual goals for water use. This is similar to the "idea" in Jones's idea-area chain and the "societal forces" described by Cohen and Rosenthal (1971). The latter two authors define societal forces as the "ideological influences that concern the organization and goals of the social lives of large aggregations of persons." For Jones (1954) the "idea" is any political idea which allows an individual's actions to be taken into account. This element can also be seen in the policy models discussed by Mitchell (1979).

These goals are not necessarily the goals of the majority, since single individuals or organizations often have the power to go to court and force a change in the way a specific resource is being used. Several court decisions (*Sierra Club v. Morton* 1972; *Sierra Club v. Mason* 1972) have ruled that a club or organization may bring suit on behalf of an injured member. Use of an area for recreational or other purposes by individual members may be all that is needed. If this use is interfered with, "injury" may have occurred. Also, some laws, such as the Clean Air Act (42 U.S.C. §§ 7401-7642, 1983) and the Clean Water Act (33 U.S.C. §§ 1251-1376, 1978), specifically grant individuals the right to bring suit to compel enforcement.

Although most research on the formation and articulation of such goals has been done by scientists other than geographers (Kasperson and Minghi 1969:313-317), Kasperson's (1969) model of municipal stress management is useful in examining the changing goals and values of urban managers. Although managers were specifically analyzed, the model is helpful in this analysis. Other models are discussed by Mitchell (1979).

As conceived here, societal and individual goals are formed by societal forces and individual values interacting with the environment. There is a strong linkage with the "Resource Field." If the perceived world is similar to human goals, the box is static and no change occurs. When individual or societal goals are not satisfied, a need to act arises, which may be satisfied with or without "Legal/Political Action."

For example, the first water users in the West were able to satisfy their desire for water by taking it from a stream and using it. No political action was needed. As more demand was put on this limited resource, the goals of all water users could not be satisfied. Nonpolitical action could be taken, such as bringing water from further away, but this was expensive and required cooperation between individuals. To insure individual rights and to resolve conflicting societal goals, laws were necessary.

The impetus for creating these laws was the California gold rush, where miners found traditional water law inappropriate (McGowen 1956). The result was the legal concept known as the appropriation doctrine, which will be discussed in Chapter 4. Briefly, this doctrine gave a water right to anyone who intended to divert water from a watercourse, actually diverted it, and applied it to a beneficial use. The first person to do this established a priority right which was superior to all rights established afterwards. Today, the appropriation doctrine is generally administered by state agencies who issue permits.

Process and Structure

The kind of political or legal action that can be taken is controlled by existing processes and structures. Political structure at the national level has frequently been discussed by geographers and has often formed a major segment in political geography texts (Norris and Haring 1980; Pounds 1972). Internal political structure has become more important (Bergman 1975; Brunn 1974; Massam 1972; Morrill 1973, 1981; Pearcy 1973; Sauer 1918; Soja 1971) and must be understood before resource use can be explained. Cohen and Rosenthal (1971) recognized this and included a hierarchy of administrative centers within the internal organization of the state.

In the United States four levels in the land use decision process have been recognized: private, local, state, and federal (Platt 1976). This is true for the use of water and other resources as well. If the private sector is excluded, the remaining levels form a hierarchy of overlapping administrative areas. Federal agencies might not control the same subject matter or territory as those at the state and local levels. For example, the Idaho Department of Water Resources, the Idaho Department of Health and Welfare, the Clearwater National Forest, the Environmental Protection Agency, and the Lewiston, Idaho Planning Commission have an interest in controlling the Clearwater River. Neither the subject matter authority nor the goals of these agencies is the same. The territory over which they have authority is also different.

Control over resource use within the United States is divided between the executive, legislative, and judicial branches of the government. All three branches exist at federal, state, and local levels with overlapping authority over the same territory. The court structure will be used to illustrate this point. For example, the Federal District Court for Idaho has jurisdiction over the same territory as the Supreme Court of the State of Idaho but not over the same subject matter. A local court has jurisdiction over a limited area, but this jurisdiction is not exclusive since the state supreme court and federal district court may also have authority. In some instances a specific lawsuit affecting resource use could be brought in either a federal or a state court. Interestingly, once a case is in court, legal issues related to the decision will be resolved even if they are ones usually decided by another court.

The United States Supreme Court has jurisdiction over all territory in the United States (Wright 1976). Beneath it are the twelve courts of appeals (circuit courts) which have regional jurisdiction as is seen in Figure 4. Federal district courts can control an area the size of a state, although in larger states there may be several districts. Figure 5 shows the division of federal district court jurisdictions.

At the state level, the trial court structure varies considerably, with many courts having limited powers based on such factors as whether the case is civil or criminal in nature, the amount of money involved, or a person's age. These factors determine whether a case is brought in small claims court, juvenile court, probate court, criminal court, or traffic court, for example. Appeal from these courts may go to an intermediate appellate court, a state supreme court, or even the U.S. Supreme Court *(Thompson v. City of Louisville* 1960).

Executive and legislative bodies have similar limitations on the area within which their power may be exercised. At the federal, state, and local levels overlapping authority over territory creates a complex regulatory structure. The structure of these internal administrative areas has been studied by geographers, but more work needs to be done on the conflicts these overlaps create.

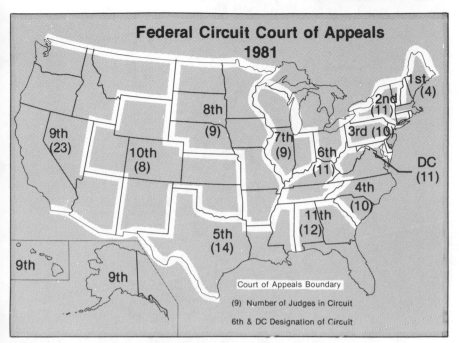

FIGURE 4 CIRCUIT COURT JURISDICTIONS (23 U.S.C. §§ 41 & 44, 1983 supp.)

To achieve the political or legal action desired, the correct functional unit at the proper level of government must be approached. The desire to obtain municipal water services would not usually be satisfied with a letter to a United States Senator or the Bureau of Land Management. The acquisition of water rights is generally controlled by state law, not federal. However, federal law may influence the use and disposal of the water as well as the amount available. The structure of the United States political system is divided into an overlapping series of administrative areas based on function and scale. These administrative areas have boundaries which can be delimited, and for any one spot, many agencies or courts will have power. Within each level of authority different political or legal processes occur which may influence decision making.

"Process" includes the formal procedures and informal processes that must occur in order to obtain a desired "goal" through "political/legal action." Formal procedures are those that are required by law while informal processes are other legal/political activities that are influential. The differences between the formal institutional arrangements used by society to resolve conflicts and the informal ones are considerable. For example, there is a field of study in law called 'Procedure' which is based on the technical steps necessary to bring a case to court and through the appeal process. Failure to follow proper legal procedure may influence the final outcome. Also, informal processes, such as the demeanor of a witness, influence the final decision.

If a legislative change is desired, there are formal procedures that must be followed to introduce a bill. Whether a bill is made law may also depend on informal processes such as lobbying. A change in legislation could occur by challenging its

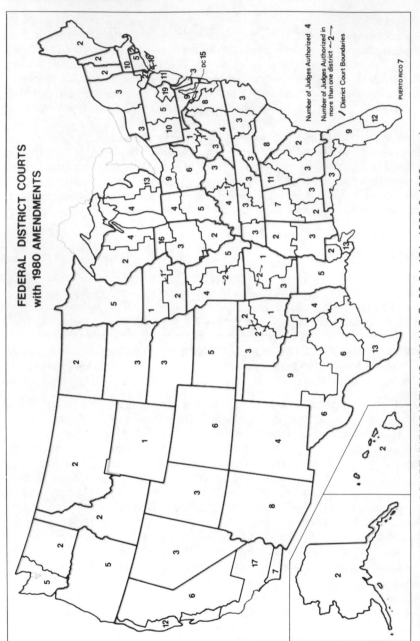

FIGURE 5   DISTRICT COURT JURISDICTIONS (28 U.S.C. §§ 81-131, 1968 & 1983 supp.)

validity in court. The formal procedures used to change the law are different from those used in introducing a bill, but the results may be the same. Informal processes such as the persuasiveness of an expert witness may be the same in front of a judge or Senate committee. The role of geographers as expert witnesses has been discussed by Mitchell (1978). However, not all informal processes operate in courts and legislative bodies. The influence of a lobbyist on legislators can be considerable, but generally there is no role for them in a court of law. There, the persuasiveness of a lawyer in an adversarial situation forms the basis of the decision.

Ideas or goals do not instantly become laws since formal procedures and informal processes control the activities that occur within the political structure. Although process and structure are developed as a result of societal values, changes in these values are influenced by structure and process, creating a circular relationship.

Although structure and process vary spatially and must be understood by geographers, these elements of the model do not affect resources except through political/legal action, the third major element in the model.

Political/Legal Action

Forms of "political/legal action" (decisions) are listed in the model. Not all political action will influence resource use in the same way. Also, the type of political/legal action will depend on the structure and processes of the political unit that formed the decision as well as individual and societal goals.

If a change in the way water is used is desired, it may be accomplished by formal or informal action. Formal action implements existing law or creates new law through judicial or legislative action. This may take many forms and more than one method may be attempted to resolve an issue. If the legislature fails to change an existing law, it may be challenged in a court on a variety of grounds. The decision by the court is a formal action creating law. Court decisions, congressional legislation, treaties, constitutions, administrative agency rules, city ordinances, and initiatives are laws which result from formal action.

Informal actions are those decisions that do not create laws but may have influence on resources, as is shown by the small arrow in the model between informal action and the resource field. These actions include voting for a representative, administrative activities, lobbying, holding hearings, congressional investigations, or inaction. Informal action may influence resource use through persuasion rather than compulsion. For example, a Senate hearing on a resource issue may point to problems that are voluntarily corrected. An agency's interpretation of existing regulations may carry weight, but may not be binding since it can be challenged in a court. The informal action may be a vote on a bill which does not succeed in creating a law. This may change the way resources are used because resource managers could be influenced to change their policies even though the law did not pass. The decision to do nothing or to change nothing must also be accepted as political action. The failure of a bill to pass is a decision which indicates that no change in resource use is desired or that there is insufficient support for change at that time.

Informal actions may eventually result in formal action. An example of this is the election of representatives to serve in legislative bodies. This is informal because no law is created. The action — voting — results in the election of a representative who becomes part of the political structure with the power to participate in formal decision making.

An election may influence the resource field without any formal action. For example, the 1980 election of President Reagan signified a change in philosophy toward resource use. Changes in the resource field have occurred without formal political action being taken. This can be seen in the political philosophy of a Secretary of the Interior which influences the way decisions are made at the lower levels within his department. Changes in the way public lands are managed result from informal actions taken by the Secretary.

There is considerable geographic research on the linkage between informal political actions and the structure and process within a political system. Most of this has been within the broad study of electoral geography. The structure of voting districts has been addressed in articles on gerrymandering and on redistricting (Morrill 1981). Electoral districts are part of the political structure, and voter decisions in them have been examined (Cox 1968; Gudgin & Taylor 1979; Johnston 1979, 1980a; Lewis 1965; Minghi and Rujley 1978; O'Loughlin 1980; Prescott 1959b; Roberts and Rummage 1965; Taylor and Johnston 1979; Wolfe and Burghardt 1978). Other informal decisions have not, perhaps because of the difficulties in collecting information and evaluating it. Although there is some research in geography on formal political actions (Beard 1975; Fitzsimmons 1980; King 1978; Martin 1930; Thorton and Koepke 1981), there is room for more research in this area since the variation in existing laws is important in understanding variations in human activities.

There are two basic kinds of law in common law countries like the United States — legislation and case law. Legislation, broadly defined, consists of such things as treaties, executive orders, bills passed by congressional bodies, ordinances passed by city councils, constitutions, as well as administrative and court rules. Case law is made up of the judicial decisions of local, state, federal, and administrative courts (Roalfe 1965).

Case law may affect only a few people in an area, impact the entire population, or change the area's political structure. The Supreme Court decision that established the principle of "one man, one vote" changed the structure of election districts (*Reynolds v. Sims* 1964). For this reason the model shows an arrow from formal political action to political process and structure. Also, the Supreme Court has at times established societal goals based on its interpretation of the constitution. The Supreme Court in *Brown v. Board of Education* (1954) held segregation violated the equal protection clause of the constitution. Although this decision did not immediately change the philosophy of society, integration became the only acceptable goal short of amending the Constitution. Since the Constitution of the United States is supreme (Article VI), it supersedes all contrary laws.

Often times the language in a statute is not clear. When this happens the courts may be asked for an interpretation. If the interpretation does not reflect legislative intent, the statute may be amended. However, even if it does reflect the intent of the legislative body, significant societal pressure against the court decision may result in amendment. For example, the United States Supreme Court's interpretation of the Endangered Species Act literally stopped construction of the Tellico Dam in Tennessee (*TVA v. Hill* 1978). Although a court's interpretation is the final word on the meaning of a law, its ruling may not be the final word on an issue. In regard to the Tellico dam, pressure occurred both from within Congress and from lobbying groups to change the law. The result was the amendment of the Endangered Species Act (16 U.S.C. § 1536, 1983 supp.) and the completion of the Tellico Dam.

Court decisions do not always clarify how the law is to be applied even when the actual statement by the court is clear. Many decisions have established that in the eastern United States the owners of land adjacent to a river have a common right to use its waters as long as the use is reasonable. The law is easy to state, but applying it to a specific situation can be difficult. Reasonableness depends on the trade-offs inherent in each situation. What is a reasonable use in one place may not be in another.

Area of Jurisdiction

In international law, jurisdiction encompasses the rights to both prescribe (create) and to enforce a rule of law (Restatement Second, Foreign Relations Law of the United States, 1965). These two rights may be separate or combined. A country may have the power to prescribe a law but not enforce it. A law may require a country's citizens to file income tax returns, but this law may not be enforceable against a citizen living abroad. A law cannot be enforced if there is no power to prescribe. For example, the United States constitution prohibits laws that would take property without compensation. A law that did this would not be enforceable if it were challenged in a court.

The power of a country to enforce laws is based on territory, nationality, the protection of state interests, and the protection of certain universal interests. Nationality (citizenship) and territory are the most important. The United States can prescribe laws over its citizens anywhere in the world, although they may not be enforceable. Jurisdiction over territory is limited by national boundaries. When dealing with a country like the United States, internal boundaries are important also because of the over-lapping hierarchy of political units. Boundaries are part of the structure of a political unit and could be considered in that part of the model as well as under jurisdiction. They are included here because of the importance of territorial jurisdiction to the enforcement of laws.

Geographers have long been interested in boundaries. There is a large body of general literature devoted to them (Hartshorne 1936; Johnson 1917; Jones 1945, 1959). There are studies of internal boundaries (Bowman 1923; Cushing 1920; Martin 1930; Mayer 1964; Prescott 1959a; Thomas 1949, 1952) and international boundaries (Ahmad 1953; Alexander 1953; Deasy 1942; Hartshorne 1933; Hill 1965; House 1959; Jones 1945; MacGrath 1927). Ocean boundaries have also been of particular interest to geographers (Alexander 1967, 1968, 1979; Boggs 1937; Capone & Ryan 1973; Hodgson & Smith 1979; Pearcy 1959; Smith 1981). Many of these works address the issue of the location of boundaries, but few look at the internal conflicts created as a result of overlapping territorial jurisdiction.

The limit of jurisdiction is not always the legal boundary around the political unit. This has been pointed out with regard to international law, but it also happens internally. For example, cities often have the power to declare certain activities a public nuisance within three miles of their boundaries, or they may have the power to veto subdivisions one mile outside of the city limit (Idaho Code § 50-334, 1980). This extraterritorial power is limited to those purposes specified by the state and within the power of the state to grant.

Extraterritorial power can also be asserted at the federal level. Countries may claim jurisdiction over their own citizens no matter where they are located. In the Endangered Species Act (16 U.S.C. § 1538, 1974), all citizens of the United States are prohibited from harming listed species anywhere in the world. If a citizen harms a listed species while in Africa, he may be prosecuted under the provisions of the Act when he returns to United States territory.

Even within the boundary of a political unit there may not be exclusive jurisdiction. For example, any one spot in the United States may be subject to the jurisdiction of local, state, and federal bodies, as is illustrated by Figure 6. Each of these government bodies may have limits on the type of power they have within a given territory. For example, federal courts do not usually have subject matter jurisdiction over local criminal violations. The authority of the legislature is limited to those things enumerated in the constitution. When a conflict between state and federal legislation or administrative rules occurs, it is resolved (as shown in Figure 7) in accordance with constitutional principles and grants of authority. This does not mean that federal statutes always supersede state statutes. This occurs only if there is a conflict. If the constitution dictates that state law should control, then it will. Here there is no conflict between the state and federal law because there is no authority for the federal law under the constitution.

Resource Field

The resource field is the area influenced by the political action. This is like Cohen and Rosenthal's (1971) 'political action area' and Jones' (1954) 'field.' The resource field may be larger or smaller than the area over which the political unit has jurisdiction.

The area affected may be smaller than the legal jurisdiction because all land is not treated in the same way. A city might create zones which place unequal restrictions on land use within the city. If the federal government owns land within the city, the city may not regulate it in all ways. Futhermore, the federal government could pass legislation that under the supremacy clause supersedes certain local regulations regardless of the ownership of land. This unequal treatment of resources within a specific political unit may be a policy decision or may result from conflicts between overlapping political units.

Level of Authority \ Type of Law	Legislation	Administrative Rules	Court Decision
Local	City Ordinance County Code City Charter	Agency Regulation: Zoning Board Building Inspection Etc.	Municipal Court District Court
State	State Statutes State Constitution	Agency Regulation: Dept. of Land Dept. of Water Resources Etc.	State Appellate Court State Supreme Court
Federal	U.S. Constitution U.S. Statutes	Agency Regulation: Dept. of Interior Dept. of Agr. Etc	U.S. District Court U.S. Circuit Court of Appeals U.S. Supreme Court

FIGURE 6   OVERLAPPING JURISDICTIONS

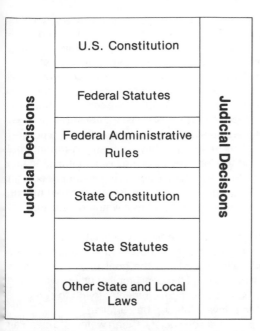

FIGURE 7   CONFLICT OF LAWS

Political action may influence the use of resources outside the area over which the governing body has jurisdiction. A new law which subsidizes agricultural commodities that are normally imported may influence distributional patterns and spatial relationships outside the political unit. Cohen and Rosenthal (1971) distinguish between political action areas and political areas. In their model the political area is the area of jurisdiction and the political action area is similar to the resource field.

The results of legal/political action on the resource field can be divided into three types. One is the effect on the landscape. This has a long history in geographic literature and is usually limited to visible impacts (Christopher 1971; Fuller 1976; Hornbeck 1979; Pattison 1957; Pryde 1976; Rice 1978; and Whittlesey 1935). It includes land ownership patterns, architectural design controls, and the reclamation of mined land. There are few changes more dramatic than those resulting from the construction of a dam and the opening of newly irrigated farm land. The Homestead Act (30 U.S.C. § § 1201-1328, 1971 supp.), the Reclamation Act (43 U.S.C. § § 371-615, 1964) and the Louisiana constitutional provision preserving the French Quarter in New Orleans (Art.14 sec. 221) are examples of laws that impact the landscape.

Specific effects on the landscape are usually limited to the area of jurisdiction of the political unit. However, since landscape features may be slow to change, they may continue to exist long after the boundary or the law has changed. This has long been known at the national level (Whittlesey 1935), but it also exists at the local level. When zones are created that exclude certain pre-existing activities, newly prohibited uses may continue as nonconforming uses with a limited form of legal protection. Also, reclamation laws in a state may only apply to future mining activities. Existing land-scape features that resulted from past mining may persist for an indefinite period.

The distributional patterns and spatial relationships of resources are also affected by legal actions. These patterns and relationships are defined by Cohen and Rosenthal (1971:30) as "existing pathways that the distribution of a phenomenon takes from place to place(s), and to the linkages in space that the distributed phenomenon has with pertinent related phenomena." Tariffs, food import restrictions, and severance taxes are examples of laws that influence linkages outside the formal jurisdiction of a political unit. The interstate highway system — the result of a law — changed the internal patterns and linkages in resource use. At the local level zoning laws control land use and transportation (King 1978; Pryde 1976; Platt 1976). Subsidizing water projects for agricultural uses affects the pattern of water use that would exist under a free market economy. Governmental action to enchance or inhibit interbasin water transfers is also a factor (Loeffler 1970; Quinn 1968).

The use of the resource itself can be directly controlled by political action. This is easy to see with local land use controls. Also, it can be observed in water use. The federal government passed the Clean Water Act with the goal of zero pollution. Western states have passed statutes which control the consumptive use of water and regulate the uses to which water may be put. Local governments, trying to conserve water during droughts, have required that lawn watering be curtailed.

Changes in the resource field have an effect on society. Clean water and clean air are expensive, and as a result, the cost of goods can increase. Some industries say this is the reason for plant closures and unemployment. Whether this is true or not, it creates a force in society which can form goals that are anti-regulatory. These goals can be articulated and may become part of the political process. Political action may be taken which will result in a change in law, which in turn will result in a change in the resource field.

The remainder of this book will be devoted to the laws controlling a shared resource — surface water.

3

Public Use of Rivers and Lakes

Although the term 'navigable' is usually used to refer to the ability of water to float boats, in the legal community the term has other meanings. The division of inland, nontidal waters into 'navigable' and 'non-navigable' classes is one way of distinguishing between 'public' and 'private' water bodies and water uses. The first part of this chapter will examine how this law developed, with the remainder devoted to public use of the water surface, ownership of the bed of a water body, and the federal navigational servitude.

Since the definition of navigable water sets limitations on public and private rights, different definitions were developed to satisfy divergent societal goals. As a result, the definition of navigable water for determining who owns the bed may be different from that which allows the public a right to use the water surface, or that which determines what water may be open for 'commercial' uses. This can create confusing results.

In the United States, the beds of navigable streams or lakes may be owned by the states and held in trust for their citizens. Under this public ownership concept, states may license uses of the bed or lease rights to minerals found there. The right of the public to water-ski over the bed can be asserted because there is a federal navigational servitude or because the state has an expanded definition of navigability which allows more public uses than exist under federal law.

The Development of 'Navigability'

Most legal systems consider certain water bodies and their beds to be public. According to MacGrady (1975), the concept of 'publicness' was attached to all property in primitive society. Thus all land and water belonged collectively to the community. Even with the development of the concept of private property, some rivers and lakes were so valuable to the public they never went into private hands. Predecessors to the United States law emerged in Rome, France, Spain, and England.

One of the oldest existing written laws to distinguish between public and private rivers is the systematic compilation ordered by the Emperor Justinian in 528. Known as the Corpus Juris Civilis (Thomas 1975), this compilation of Roman laws contains clues to the difference between public and private rights, but it lacks complete clarity on the subject.

Although in one place there is a statement that all rivers are public (*Institutes* 2.1.2, ...d in Sandars 1970), brooks and what we would call intermittent rivers were ...cluded from the definition (*Digest* 43.12.1.3, found in Ware 1905). A "brook" was ...aced in the excluded category because of its small size or because the adjacent land ...wners felt the waterbody should be excluded (*Digest* 43.12.1.1). Interference with navigation or landings on a public river was prohibited. The rights to fish, use the river banks, and use the river itself were common rights.

Although there is some confusion over who *owned* the river water, bed, and banks, MacGrady (1975) has concluded that the beds of public rivers were owned by the state and those of brooks and intermittent rivers by the adjacent riparian landowner. All river banks were owned by the adjacent landowner, but the public could use the banks of non-private rivers. Flowing water was not considered susceptible to ownership and was the property of no one in particular. Even though the water could not be owned, the riparian owner of a private river was given an exclusive right to use its flowing waters.

Also, the Romans distinguished between navigable and non-navigable rivers. Navigable rivers were regulated more stringently than others. Water could not be taken from navigable rivers or their tributaries if it would reduce their navigable capacity. Obstructions along the banks were prohibited. Under Roman law navigable rivers were those having "the capacity to be a path for commercial boating, including rafts" (MacGrady 1975:530). This is similar to one of the tests used in the United States today indicating the continuing value placed on commercial navigation.

The influence of Roman law can be seen in France and Spain. Spanish law was also influenced by the Moors. These European laws were predecessors in the development of the navigability concept in the United States because of their linkage with the Southwest and French Louisiana. The Visigoths of Spain prohibited obstructions on rivers or other inhibitions to fishing or commercial navigation (Spanish law: *Fuero Juzgo* 8.4.29).

The later Moorish influence in Spain reflects a societal response to a drier environment. Public rights were based on the need to quench human thirst and water animals. Large bodies of water owned by no one were open to the public. Water that was appropriated and belonged to a group or an individual was open to the public only in extreme need or by paying for it. Wells and springs dug on public land were regulated according to the needs of the parties and the amount of labor each contributed to the development of the water.

In 1256 a compilation of the laws of Castile was ordered by Alfonso the Wise. Known as *Las Siete Partidas*, it took nine years to complete. Other codes and collections of law have been compiled since then, but the original is still considered valuable in interpreting today's laws. In *Las Siete Partidas* public rivers must be permanent and flow into the ocean (MacGrady 1975). The Texas Supreme Court relied on this Spanish law in several cases (*Manry v. Robison* 1932; *State v. Grubstake Inv. Ass'n.* 1927; *Templar* 1980a). A California case (*Lux v. Haggin* 1886) stated that under Spanish law all navigable streams were public, but not all public streams were navigable. As with Roman law, navigable rivers were given greater protection by prohibiting the removal of water which could interfere with navigation.

Until 1804 France did not have a unified body of law. The creation of the French Civil Code supplanted a confusing array of feudal, church, and national laws. The code states that all floatable streams are public. This is a departure from Roman and Spanish law and seems to limit the public's interest in water bodies to those that are 'navigable in fact.' This concept is based on the idea of actually being able to float on the river for commercial purposes. However, this has been expanded so that all streams listed through a series of administrative actions are also considered public (MacGrady 1975). The beds of public streams are owned by the state and those of private streams are privately owned (Wiel 1919). As in Roman law, the public has a right to all flowing water, but this right does not allow passage along non-public streams.

English Common Law

The Roman concept of publicness spread to many parts of Europe and was recognized in England. Later, Roman Law concepts were rejected and by the end of King John's reign in 1216, the title to most riverbeds had been granted to individuals (MacGrady 1975). Private ownership of river beds must have been well accepted in feudal England because there are no records of legal controversies over them during this time. Bed ownership did not mean that the riparian owners had complete control, however, because the Magna Carta (Chapter 22, found in Stingham 1966) required that all the permanent fish-weirs be removed from the Thames River so that navigation could occur.

Beginning around 1600 there was a series of cases on fishing rights and bed ownership in the English courts. Feudalism was breaking down and the rules governing property were beginning to change. Two different concepts evolved in the courts on the publicness of rivers. In one, rivers had to be affected by the ebb and flow of the tide before they were public, and in the other they had to be 'navigable in fact.'

In 1631 an English court (*Attorney General v. Philpot*) held that the crown owned all the land under waters which were subject to the ebb and flow of the tide. This decision was an extension of the principle of crown ownership of land beneath the sea — if the crown owned that land, then it must also own the land that was periodically covered by the sea. This case was ignored in most subsequent decisions, however, because the judges who had decided the case were later impeached for corruption.

Although the case was ignored, the 'tidal' concept soon began to be accepted. In 1674 *Lord Fitzwalter's Case* recognized the public's right to fish on water influenced by the tide. However, a 1703 decision (*Warren v. Matthews*) only recognized a right to fish in all 'navigable' waters. Both concepts were used to determine bed ownership (*Rex v. Smith* 1780; *Le Roy v. Trinity House* 1662) until the issue was finally resolved in 1868 (*Murphy v. Ryan*). Today tidality indicates crown ownership of the bed. With this ownership goes the right to fish, but it does not extend to rivers that can be navigated. On them there is a public right of navigation, but the bed is privately owned.

Early United States Law

The concepts of tidality and navigability were brought to the United States as part of its common law tradition. At the time the United States gained independence, English courts had not reached a final solution for determining public rights. Thus, the conclusions of the United States courts on this issue were independent of the subsequent English decisions.

In common law systems, courts can make laws that resolve disputes between individuals as well as address societal goals. The decision settling a dispute between two individuals serves as law in all similar instances within that jurisdiction. All people are affected even if there has been no generally recognized need at a societal level. Since state and federal courts have jurisdiction over the same territory, conflicting common law definitions of 'navigable' developed.

Several landmark decisions were especially important in developing the current concepts. When the United States Supreme Court decided in *Martin v. Waddell* (1842), the 'public trust doctrine' was formed, with the states owning the submerged land under navigable water bodies for the 'common use' of the public. As a result, the state of New Jersey became the owner of some mud flats in the Raritan River. Under English common law no such doctrine had ever been recognized. Nevertheless, the court stated that under English common law, land beneath navigable waters was "held by the king as a public trust." The actual source of this doctrine was an 1821 New Jersey case (*Arnold v. Mundy*) in which the judge had apologized for rendering a hasty decision.

Thus, the public trust doctrine was created by an obscure state court judge in response to what he perceived public policy should be and not by following English common law. This decision was followed by the United States Supreme Court, and the ownership of many acres of submerged land was declared public with public rights to control their use. This law was not created by public pressure, but in resolving a dispute between individuals. If there had been public support to create this policy, then legislation would have been appropriate. If there is no attempt to pass a law which would overturn the judicial decision, it may stand as a reflection of the goals or desires of society. It may also continue as law because it is unimportant to society.

Subsequent state and federal laws were created which also define navigability and control resource use.

Federal 'Navigational Servitude'

The public's interest in water can be exercised under the concept of a 'navigational servitude.' The navigational servitude prohibits activities inconsistent with commercial navigation (*United States v. Rands* 1967). The doctrine originally created a public right of way over a stream or lake regardless of ownership of the bed and banks. It prohibits obstructions to navigation. This control may be exercised without compensating adjacent property owners for interference with their claimed rights. The following example illustrates this concept (*Wilbour v. Gallagher* 1969).

Lake Chelan is a navigable lake in Washington state (Figure 8). Its natural water line is 1,079 feet above sea level; a small dam constructed in 1927 permits alteration of this level. In May of each year the dam is closed, so that the water rises 21 feet above the natural level by June 15. The water stays at that level until September when the dam is opened. Land along part of the lake had been conveyed to private parties prior to the construction of the dam. From late spring through the fall some of this land is covered with water. One property owner decided to fill in his waterfront to a height of 1105 feet so the area submerged each summer would remain above water. This increased the amount of usable land, but it interfered with the neighboring owners. The Washington Supreme court held that the area between the 1079 and 1100 feet levels was:

> ". . . subjected to the rights of navigation, together with its incidental rights of fishing, boating, swimming, water skiing, and other related recreational purposes generally regarded as corollary to the right of navigation and the use of public waters. When the level of the lake is lowered so that the defendants' land is no longer submerged, then they

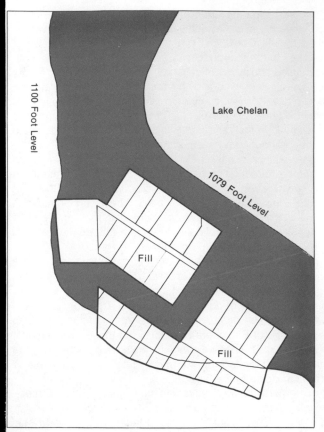

FIGURE 8   LAKE CHELAN *(Wilbour v. Gallagher* 1969)

are entitled to keep trespassers off their land, and may do with the land
as they wish consistent with the right of navigation when it is submerged.
   It follows that the defendants' fills, insofar as they obstruct the sub-
mergence of land at or below the 1100 foot level, must be removed. The
court cannot authorize or approve an obstruction to navigation" (Wilbour
v. Gallagher 1969:239; citations omitted).

The United States Supreme Court refused to hear this case on appeal.
   As this example clearly demonstrates, the navigational servitude grants the public
a right to use navigable waters no matter who owns the bed. Obstructions to navigation
will not be allowed. However, the right is not absolute, and it does not extend to all the
waters that may be regulated under the commerce clause. This means that the public
does not have a right of free use everywhere. There may be some uses for which
owners must be compensated before the public use is allowed. This was demonstrated
in a recent United States Supreme Court decision (*Kaiser Aetna v. United States*
1979).
   The Kaiser Aetna Co. wished to construct a residential-marina subdivision on a
lagoon in Hawaii called Kuapa Pond. The lagoon was considered private property

under Hawaiian law. Since it was separated from the ocean by a barrier beach, a channel was needed to connect the two. On applying for a permit to excavate a passage they were informed by the Corps of Engineers that the lagoon was not navigable and no permit was needed. Although there was some tidal influence within the lagoon, the old test which used tidality in defining navigability was ignored by the majority. Millions of dollars were spent dredging the lagoon and constructing the channel. Upon completion, the development company was informed that the lagoon was now navigable and could be used by the public. The government brought suit claiming the lagoon was 'navigable in fact' and under this standard the public could have access to the water body without compensating the owner.

The federal district court hearing the case held (*United States v. Kaiser Aetna* 1976) that the lagoon was subject to regulation by the Corps of Engineers, but there was no navigational servitude which would give the public access. Before the right could be granted, reasonable compensation must be paid. The Court of Appeals (*United States v. Kaiser Aetna* 1978) reversed this decision, holding that when private land is converted into a waterway which is 'navigable in fact,' a federal navigational servitude is also created. The United States Supreme Court disagreed.

The Supreme Court recognized, as did the district court, that water may be considered navigable for regulatory purposes but not for a navigational servitude. In deciding public access was to be denied unless compensation was paid, the court reasoned that the expenditure of millions of dollars had created expectancies in the minds of the developers which would be destroyed if the navigational servitude was upheld. The statement by the Corps of Engineers had bolstered those expectations, and the agency decision to allow public access was unfair to the developer because the lagoon had always been treated as private property under state law. The state had never extended public recreation rights to the lagoon.

The dissenting opinion disagreed in several ways with the majority. The dissenters thought the lagoon was navigable in its natural state because it was affected by the ebb and flow of the tide — the oldest of the navigation tests. If this argument had been accepted, it would have controlled the entire decision. Second, the navigational servitude includes "privately created or enhanced waters." Also, water covered under the navigational servitude is the same as that of the commerce clause. Since the water could be regulated under the commerce clause it is navigable and no compensation should be due. Finally, since a state could not create an interest superior to the federal navigational servitude, it did not matter what the state law said about the ownership of the bed.

The effect of the Kaiser Aetna decision limits the public's right of access to water not navigable in its natural state but made so by private funds. If there has been navigation in the past, then there is a navigational servitude. In this case the investor relied on the government's statement, and a large amount of private money was spent with the expectation that use of the water would remain private. Thus, the limitations on the navigational servitude may exist only when large sums are spent in reliance upon government statements. Also, this exception may not exist where the state has extended prior public rights to the water. Even if these conditions are not met, public access can be obtained if just compensation is paid.

A navigational servitude is not the only public right to the use of water. Under a variety of state laws and court decisions, others have been created.

Bed Ownership

Under state law the public's right to float on rivers or lakes is often limited to those waters where the state owns the bed. The original thirteen states obtained title to the beds of all rivers and lakes that were considered navigable. The states were considered to be the successors to whatever interest the English Crown possessed. The Supreme Court (*Martin v. Waddell* 1842) established this interest even though the legal issue in England had not been resolved when the United States was formed.

Since all new states created from federal territory were admitted on an equal footing with the original thirteen, they also received title to the beds of navigable water bodies (*Pollard's Lessee v. Hagen* 1845). This doctrine does not apply to Texas and Hawaii because they were independent when they joined the Union. However, they may claim ownership based on their own laws which existed during independence. West Virginia and Maine were formed from the territory of the original states and obtained title to the beds in the same way as those states (Davis 1978a). Whether a state retains title to the bed after statehood is a function of state law (*Hardin v. Jordan* 1891).

Before the states outside the original thirteen colonies were formed, the federal government had title to the beds of navigable water bodies in those federal territories and had the power to convey the bed to an individual. An individual's ownership of a bed which was obtained before the territory became a state was not affected by the onset of statehood (*Brewer-Elliot Oil & Gas Co. v. United States* 1922; *Shively v. Bowlby* 1894). Similarly, before the United States had sovereignty over territory, the prior sovereign may have conveyed the title to the bed to an individual. In such instances the federal government could not give the state title to the bed because the prior sovereign had already conveyed them (*Knight v. U.S. Land Association* 1891). For this reason courts in the Southwest may need to look at Spanish and Mexican law in determining bed ownership.

On non-navigable streams the title to the bed went with the adjacent upland owner. Bed ownership was connected with the concept of navigability, but what did 'navigability' mean? Prior to a series of cases between 1922 and 1931, state courts defined navigability as they chose, as did federal courts. Since these definitions were often inconsistent, it was unclear who owned the beds wherever they conflicted. A considerable body of literature in the legal periodicals has developed on this (Comment 1977b; Commentary 1977; Davis 1978a; Gibson 1976; Johnson & Austen 1967; Leighty 1970; MacGrady 1975; Note 1979).

The Federal Test

Prior to the 1920s the United States Supreme Court had not addressed the question of whether federal or state tests for navigability should control the question of bed ownership. In three precedent-setting cases (*Brewer-Elliot Oil Co. v. United States* 1922; *United States v. Holt State Bank* 1926; *United States v. Utah* 1931), the Court decided the federal test would be used to determine which streams were navigable at the time a state was admitted to the Union. These formal court actions created new law which influences resource use today. How this law evolved will be examined below.

The early federal court decisions on navigability do not distinguish clearly between those cases concerned with bed ownership and those where it is defined for other purposes. The first cases (*The Daniel Ball* 1870; *The Montello* 1874) were concerned with penalizing vessels operating in navigable United States waters without licenses. This is known as navigability for admiralty purposes.

> *Those rivers must be regarded as public navigable rivers in law which are navigable in fact. And they are navigable in fact when they are used, or are susceptible of being used, in their ordinary condition, as* **highways for commerce,** *over which trade and travel are or may be conducted in the* **customary modes** *of trade and travel on water (The Daniel Ball* 1870:563; emphasis added).

The English test based on the ebb and flow of tides was rejected as the exclusive test. The courts recognized that many of the rivers actually being used for navigation in the United States were not influenced by the tides. The general rules in these cases formed the background for those on bed ownership.

Nine Supreme Court decisions form the basis for the law on the title to the beds of navigable waters (*Oregon ex. rel., State Land Board v. Corvallis* 1977; *Bonelli Cattle Co. v. Arizona* 1973; *Utah v. United States* 1971; *United States v. Oregon* 1935; *United States v. Utah* 1931; *United States v. Holt State Bank* 1926; *Brewer-Elliot Oil and Gas Co. v. United States* 1922; *Oklahoma v. Texas* 1922; *Packer v. Bird* 1891). Three of these have been decided since 1970. As a result, it is possible to state with clarity what the law is, but it can still be difficult to apply these standards to a specific water body.

Title to the bed passes at the time the state enters the Union and is based on the stream or lake conditions that existed at that time. This is different from definitions of navigability for other purposes, such as those that are derived under the commerce clause of the Constitution. Commerce clause definitions can include streams or water bodies that can be made navigable at some future time because of improvements (*United States v. Appalachian Electric Power Co.* 1941). The standard used for title to the bed may be difficult to apply because records on the conditions of the steam at statehood may not exist. This can create problems in presenting convincing evidence on the actual stream conditions. No one alive today remembers what rivers were like in California when it became a state in 1850. Geographers have had a role in attempting to provide this information in past cases (Bowman 1923).

Navigability for title purposes is determined by the "natural and ordinary condition" of the water. This includes rapids or rocks that make navigation difficult, but not impossible (Johnson & Austen 1967). Unlike the commerce clause cases which will be discussed later, the water body need not be navigable in 'interstate commerce.' A pair of federal cases (*Utah v. United States* 1971; *Hardy Salt Co. v. Southern Pacific Transportation Co.* 1974) have held that the Great Salt Lake, which is entirely within one state, is navigable for title purposes but not for commerce clause purposes.

The water body must also be a 'highway for commerce' capable of supporting 'customary modes of travel.' Two U.S. Supreme Court decisions illustrate this point. Mud Lake in Minnesota was three to six feet deep at the time of statehood and was used by small boats bringing supplies to merchants (*United States v. Holt State Bank* 1926). During drought periods it was difficult to use the water body. Vegetation became so dense by the end of each growing season that movement was impeded. Despite these physical hinderances, the Court found the bed of the water body to be state land. Commercial goods were actually transported on the lake and sold at the time Minnesota became a state. The size of the boats was not important.

In another case (*United States v. Oregon* 1935), the title to the beds of Malher, Harney, and Mud Lakes in south central Oregon was in question. All three of these lakes are subject to extreme fluctuations in area and depth. The largest and deepest of the lakes has covered as much as 40,000 acres, but most of this is extremely shallow. Out of the total, only 10,000 acres is deeper than three feet. Motorboats, rowboats, and canoes have been used on the lakes by duck hunters and trappers. Launching boats is difficult because they have to be dragged a long distance through the mud. The Court decided these lakes are not navigable for bed title purposes. Since they are isolated geographically and access is difficult, 'economic' travel on the lakes has not occurred. 'Customary' seems to mean the same as 'commercial' since actual commercial navigation is required at some time before a water body will be considered navigable for bed title purposes (*Utah v. United States* 1971).

Two recent circuit court decisions declare that all that is necessary to show state title is evidence that a stream was used for commercial log floating or that canoe travel occurred (*State of Oregon v. Riverfront Protective Ass'n* 1982; *North Dakota v. Andrus* 1982).

State Tests

Although the federal test for bed title controlled the rights the states received when they joined the Union, state title tests are still important. When the states received title to the beds, they had the power to keep or dispose of them. A state may or may not have retained control creating spatial variation in present bed ownership.

Before the Supreme Court decisions which required federal law to be used in determining bed ownership, there were many state court decisions. These tests are still in use today and many conflict with federal law. When they do, federal law remains the control for title purposes (under the definition of 'navigability'), but state law has been incorporated into this to determine what rights the state retains and what rights were granted to adjacent land owners. The result is a complex mix.

Some old state decisions adopted the English rule of tidality. Thus, the state kept title only where there was tidal influence. Davis (1978a) identified the following states created from federal territory that use this definition: Colorado, Illinois, Mississippi, Nebraska, and Oregon. Johnson and Austen (1967) would exclude Oregon from the list. Other states developed different standards. According to P. Davis (1978) a rule of 'navigability in fact' similar to the federal rule was adopted by Arkansas, California, Florida, Idaho, Indiana, Iowa, Louisiana, Minnesota, Missouri, Montana, Nevada, Oklahoma, Tennessee, Utah, Washington, and Wyoming. These states retained title to the beds of only those waters navigable in fact. Other approaches have been tried, such as the pleasure boat test adopted by Minnesota (*Lamprey v. Metcalf* 1893) and North Dakota (*Roberts v. Taylor* 1921). In Texas all rivers with an average width of thirty feet are navigable (Texas Code Annotated, Natural Resources § 21.001 (3), § 21,012, 1978; Templar 1980a). In Massachusetts (Mass. Gen. Law. Ann. Ch. 131 § 1 & 45, 1981), Maine (*Conant v. Jordan* 1910) and New Hampshire (N.H. Rev. Stat. Ann. § 271.20, 1977) ponds over a specified minimum size — great ponds — are public. Some states use a saw log test (*Collin v. Gerhardt* 1926).

A classification of the tests used today by different states to determine navigability for bed ownership purposes is difficult since they are not always clear. Any classification is further complicated because a state may have different tests for different purposes and may use them inconsistently. Also, differences exist in the way state courts have interpreted 'navigability in fact,' creating several possible types of conflicts between federal and state law.

Conflicts in Ownership

Before a state is created, the federal government, as sovereign, has the power to convey title to beds of navigable and non-navigable waters to private individuals. Such a conveyance would often occur in conjunction with the grant of adjacent land. If this transfer of bed ownership has not been written in the deed conveying the land, and if there is no law controlling the situation, then the transfer of the bed may be implied. Courts have held that prestatehood grants of upland areas imply a grant of title to the medial line of beds of non-navigable streams only. Ownership of the bed is not changed if the state at a later time declares the water navigable.

In Figure 9, examples **A** and **B** indicate prestatehood grant possibilities. Grant 1 in both **A** and **B** are the same. Prior to statehood, the federal government has granted individuals lands adjacent to a stream considered to be navigable for title purposes under both federal and state laws. The title to the adjacent bed remains with the federal government until statehood (*United States v. Holt State Bank* 1926), after which the state as owner has power to sell it, give it away, or regulate its use (*Barney v. Keokuk* 1876). However, this power is not exclusive and is subject to a paramount federal right of navigation. The state can do nothing which will interfere with that right.

In grant **A**-2 there has been a prestatehood grant of land that is navigable under the state test but not under the federal test. Since the grant is before statehood, federal law controls bed ownership. Unless a clause in the deed prohibits the conveyance, it will be implied that the bed of the non-navigable waters goes with the upland grant (*Hardin v. Jordan* 1891). When the state is created ownership does not change.

In grant **B**-2 the water is considered navigable under federal law but not under state law. The bed remains in federal hands until statehood. At that time, state law controls; since the water is non-navigable under state law, title extending to the medial line in the bed is recognized in the owner of **B**-2.

Where grants **A**-3 and **B**-3 were made the water is considered non-navigable under both state and federal law. Since the grants are before statehood, federal law controls; by implication the landowners' title will go to the medial line of the bed. At statehood any remaining federal interest is transferred, and the state may keep it or grant it to private parties.

Federal grants of land made after statehood have different results. Where grants **C**-1 and **D**-1 are made the river is navigable, and therefore, the bed is already under state ownership. State law controls this situation since the federal government cannot convey land in which it has no interest. The state may retain the land or dispose of it.

In example **C**-2 the bed is navigable under state law but non-navigable under federal law. State law controls how much of the stream bed is included when the federal government conveys the upland area. Federal courts use state law in deciding this issue because they have recognized the importance of keeping property law consistent within each state (*Hardin v. Jordan* 1891). In example **C**-2 the state definition of navigability for ownership purposes would prevent the adjacent property owner from being granted the bed. Some commentators say the bed would go to the state in this circumstance, but the better view is that it will be retained by the federal government (P. Davis 1978; MacGrady 1975). The court decisions on this are inconsistent.

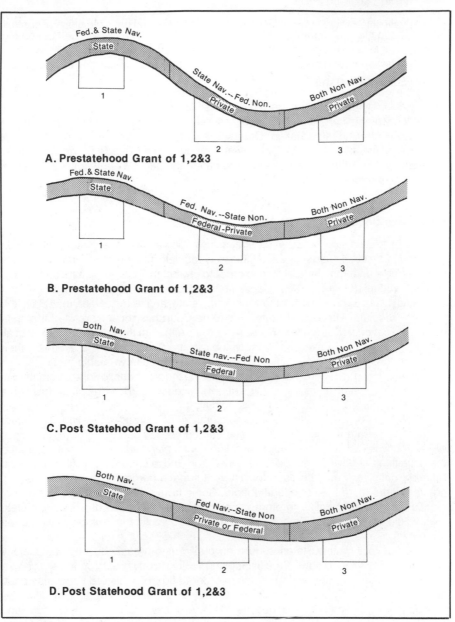

FIGURE 9   CONFLICTS IN BED OWNERSHIP

The bed is navigable under the federal test but not under the state test in grant **D**-2. At statehood the bed is granted to the state. Since state law has classified the bed as non-navigable, a problem is created. There are two possible solutions. If it is assumed that state law operates immediately at statehood, state laws will recognize ownership in the adjacent owner — the federal government. If title is not transferred at statehood, but when the federal grant is made, the bed will go to the private upland owner. There is no clear rule on when title is transferred in this situation.

If the water is non-navigable under federal and state law, the bed is private with state law controlling the situation. Grants **C**-3 and **D**-3 illustrate this point.

The ownership of the bed of a water body is only one way the concept of navigability is used. It also may be used to define the public's rights to float on water, fish, or build dams.

Public Use Under Other State Law

There are several other ways states have power over the water within their boundaries. Under its police power a state may regulate its waters, whether or not they are navigable under the federal test, in order to protect the public's health, safety, and general welfare (Leighty 1971). Some states (Colorado, Idaho, New Mexico, and Wyoming) claim ownership of all the water in the state, and as the owner, they claim the power to regulate. The United States Supreme Court has recently refuted the state ownership concept (*Sporhase v. Nebraska* 1982). Although these powers exist, not all states have chosen to exercise them to their limits. Some states have limited their control to those waters they consider navigable under bed ownership tests.

Where there is a federal navigational servitude there is a public right to commercial navigation. If the state owns the bed, it is generally considered that the public has rights to use the surface because the state is holding it in trust for the people.

State laws on public use are a complex mix of cases and legislation. The major areas of concern are whether the surface can be used, what kind of right of access exists and whether there are public shoreline rights. Many states have not separated the definitions of navigability for surface use from those used for bed title purposes. Different definitions may be used for different surface purposes, and rights may be granted under more than one legal theory. Some laws on public surface use do not mention navigability at all. Therefore, a comprehensive overview of all relevant state laws would be difficult in this book. As a result, this section will simply illustrate the diversity that exists.

The earliest United States statute on public use (Massachusetts Bay Colony Ordinance of 1641 § 2) allows "free fishing and fowling in any great ponds" and gives a right of passage over the land of others in order to do this. This ordinance has been adopted in Maine by judicial decision (*Conant v. Jordan* 1910) and modified by subsequent legislation in Massachusetts (Mass. Ann. Laws, Ch. 131 § 1§ 45, 1981 and Ch. 91, § 35, 1975) and New Hampshire (N.H. Rev. Stat. § 271.20, 1977). In Massachusetts a great pond must be more than twenty acres in size for fishing and hunting but only ten acres for other purposes. In New Hampshire and Maine great ponds are ten acres. There are many states, especially in the West and Midwest, that allow public use of waters not navigable under the federal title test.

Because of the importance of water in the West, state constitutions declare the water in the state to be owned by the public. In Idaho (*Southern Idaho Fish and Game*

Association v. Picabo Livestock Co. 1974), New Mexico (*State v. Red River Valley Co.* 1945), and Wyoming (*Day v. Armstrong* 1961) this has been used as the basis for expanding public rights in water over private beds. Colorado, with a similar constitutional provision, has restricted public rights by saying ownership applies only to the allocation of water rights and to consumptive uses. The original Colorado case interpreting the constitutional provision (*Hartman v. Tresise*) was decided in 1905, long before the expansion of public rights in other states. A more recent decision upheld this decision (*People v. Emmert* 1979).

Some states have used log floating as a criterion for determining public uses (*Watkins v. Dorris* 1901; *Moore v. Sanborne* 1853). In Idaho, navigable rivers include, among other things, those capable of floating a log in excess of six inches in diameter during the time the river carries its greatest volume (I.C. § 36.1601, 1977). In Wisconsin, if a "saw-log" can be floated to the mill at high water, the stream is considered navigable (*Nekoosa Edwards Paper Co. v. Railroad Commission* 1931). Some states, meanwhile, have specifically rejected a log floating test (Georgia Code Ann. § 44-8-5, 1982; New Hampshire Rev. Stat. Ann. § 271.9, 1977).

A pleasure boat test has been adopted in some states in recognition that recreation capability can create public rights. In some states this test may be tied to the definition of navigability, but it need not be. This is a rapidly changing area of the law. In some states the public's rights have been codified so that navigable water is defined as "all water useful for any public purpose" including logging, boating, hunting, trapping, fishing, and recreation (Alaska Statutes § 38.05.365, 1976). Idaho (I.C. § 36-1601, 1977) and Montana (Mont. Rev. Code § 87-2-305, 1983) have similar provisions; others could be added to the list.

There are public recreation rights that have been recognized by the courts without any legislation (*Bohn v. Albertson* 1951; *State v. Bollenbach* 1954; *Johnson v. Seifert* 1960; *Luscher v. Reynolds* 1936; *Lundberg v. Notre Dame* 1938). In California the public trust doctrine has been used to create recreational rights (*People v. Mack* 1971).

The confusion between recreational and log floatation definitions is illustrated by two Michigan cases. In *Kelly ex rel. MacMullen v. Hallden* (1974) the Michigan appellate court held that recreational capacity was sufficient to create public rights. In this decision the court stated that nine other states recognized this type of public right. In 1982 the Michigan Supreme Court (*Bott v. Com'n of Natural Resources, etc.*) refused to give up their log floatation test for a recreational boating test. The three to two vote on this decision exemplifies the overall controversy.

In some states there is no attempt to link the public's rights to the concept of navigability. Under the police power, for example, Indiana has declared the natural scenic beauty of Indiana's lakes a public right so they can be preserved, protected, and enjoyed as well as used for recreation (Ind. Ann. State. § 13-2-11.1-2, 1983 supp.). In Minnesota public waters include, among other things, all those determined navigable by the courts, all having more than a two square mile drainage, any with public access, and all trout streams (Minn. Stat. Ann. § 105.37, 1983 supp.).

Some states have determined that public rights exist in streams or lakes that have been surveyed under the public land survey. States that use this method of determining public rights include North Dakota (N.D. Code Ann. § 61-15-01, 1960) and Oregon (Oregon Rev. Stat. § 274.430, 1981). In some states there are historic overtones, such as the Mississippi requirement (Miss. Rev. Code Ann. § 51-1-1, 1973) that navigable streams must be 25 miles long and capable of floating a steamboat with two hundred bales of cotton for 30 consecutive days out of the year. This has recently been expanded to allow fishing on rivers five miles long, three feet deep for 90 days, with an average width of thirty feet. In Texas, streams that retain an average width of thirty feet upstream from their mouth are considered navigable (Texas Code Annotated, Natural Resources § 21.001(3), 1978), but there is considerable confusion about what that means to public rights (Templar 1980b).

There are many inconsistencies when the concept of navigability is looked at from the state level. The title to beds will initially be determined by federal law, and there is a federal navigational servitude which allows commercial uses. Other public uses will be determined by state law. Some of these are limited by the state's definition of navigable water. In some cases the public right is equal to that area covered under the federal navigational servitude, and in others it is unclear how far it will extend. For example, the Alaska Constitution provided that there would be public access to navigable waters which would be defined by legislation. It took until 1976 for Alaska to do this; the state includes all water 'navigable in fact' for any useful purpose (Alaska Stat. § 38.05.365 (22), 1976).

In many cases, the state definition of navigability is more expansive than the federal government's. This trend is increasing in order to provide the right to public recreation which society seems to be demanding. This can create conflicts because the bed of the stream or lake is in private hands.

4

The Allocation of Water Rights

Because there is a high demand for surface water, it has become necessary for society to develop a system to allocate water rights. State laws may control allocation, but individuals may own surface water outside the normal state system. Municipalities may have the same rights as individuals, but a city's right may be expanded as the city grows, whereas an individual's right may be fixed. On top of this are federal rights which may place limits on the other rights. This chapter discusses how water is allocated and how the conflicts between the different parties are resolved.

Private Water and Pueblo Rights

Although most surface water is controlled by a state allocation system, some is considered private property. Because it is difficult to control or regulate, diffused surface water is excluded from some state's systems. Also, for historic reasons some water is considered to belong to specified cities and is not subject to state control.

Diffused Surface Water

Although the hydrologic cycle is usually treated by scientists as a connected system, the law is different for each part. There are two kinds of surface water that have legal significance. One is water in rivers and lakes. The other kind hydrologists refer to as overland flow or surface runoff. This water has landed on the surface but has not infiltrated, evaporated, or reached a river or lake. In legal terms this water is usually referred to as 'diffused surface water' and may not have the same definition a hydrologist would give overland flow.

Since diffused surface water may flow into streams or lakes, anyone who interferes with it may harm existing water rights. This could occur through soil conservation practices which reduce runoff, or by intentionally capturing the water for some other use. In the West, where water shortages and sparse rainfall are common, disputes over such interferences have arisen. If the diffused surface water belongs to the landowner, he could "capture" it and do what he wants with it. If it is controlled by the holder of the stream water rights, no interference with the flow would be allowed. This might prevent soil conservation measures if it were the accepted rule.

Many court cases say diffused surface water belongs to the surface owner until it reaches a stream and thus is outside the allocation system. *State v. Hiber* (1935), as mentioned in Chapter 1, is a good example of this. In this case Mr. Hiber prevented diffused surface water from flowing onto another's land. Since he was considered the owner of the water by the Wyoming Supreme Court he had a right to do this. Other cases that define a stream's extent concur (*Maricopa County, etc., v. Southwest Cotton Co.* 1931; *Tierney v. Yakima County* 1925; *LeMunyon v. Gallitin Valley Ry. Co.* 1921; *Hutchinson v. Watson Slough Ditch Co.* 1909; *Simmons v. Winters* 1891; *Lux v. Haggin* 1886).

In some western states, water subject to state control is defined by statute or constitution. In North Dakota (No. Dak. Cent. Code § 61-01-01, 1960) and Arizona (Ariz. Rev. Stat. § 45-101 (6), 1983 supp.) diffused surface waters are excluded from the definition of water. In Colorado (Colo. Const. Art. 16, § 5) only "natural" streams are subject to state law, and in New Mexico (N. Mex. Const. art 16, § 2) the state controls "every natural stream, perennial or torrential."

On the other hand, Nevada (Nev. Rev. Stat. § 533.025, 1978), Oregon (Ore. Com. Rev. Stat. § 537.110, 1981) and Utah (Utah Code Ann. § 73-1-1, 1980) statutes say that state law controls all water. There are several Utah cases that interpret this to include diffused surface water (*McNaughton v. Eaton* 1952; *Riordan v. Westwood* 1949). Concurring in one opinion a justice includes rain and snow as public water regardless of where it falls. Public ownership would start from the moment the moisture strikes land. In Montana (Mont. Rev. Code § 85-2-103, 1983) diffused surface water is specifically included under public waters.

If diffused surface water is owned by the landowner, what happens when an entire watershed is owned? Oklahoma City owned almost all the land in the East Elm Creek watershed. When it built a dam the city claimed ownership of all the water that flowed into the reservoir. It said it had only captured diffused surface water which belonged to it. The Oklahoma Supreme Court held (*Oklahoma Water Res. Bd. v. Central Okl. Master Conservancy Dist.* 1969) that the city had not captured diffused surface water since the water had been in a river before the dam was built. Once water is in a river or lake it is subject to the control of state law. State law generally treats lakes the same as streams. However, when does water become part of a stream?

Bed, Banks, and Flow

In general, a river or water course has a channel with a bed and banks. Also, it has a current or reasonably regular flow of water. This may be easy to state, but what about a braided stream — does it have banks? What about stream channels that have water in them only two or three times a year after a heavy rain? What about a stream that disappears underground and reappears as a spring? Is it in a channel with bed and banks while it is underground?

When the bed and banks are clearly visible, their existence is generally accepted. Draws or swales do serve as routes for water drainage, but they are not necessarily water courses in a legal sense. Vegetation must be considered. If an area is entirely grass covered, this weighs against its being a water course. If it can be crossed easily in a vehicle because it has no banks, this must also be considered (*State v. Hiber* 1935). Since the bed and banks are visible features, this often can be resolved easily. However, there are exceptions.

Medano Creek in Colorado disappears into some sand hills near Zapato. Three and seven miles west of where it goes underground two springs appear. In 1902 two people began using water from the creek, and the flow in the springs was reduced. Prior appropriators of the spring water, who could no longer get their full appropriation, sued those taking water from the creek. Can underground water be a water course subject to state law since it is moving under the surface through sand? The Colorado Supreme Court held (*Medano Ditch Co. v. Adams* 1902) that even though no channel was visible, it was well defined and known. Therefore, no interference was allowed with the appropriated rights.

Other cases have been concerned with the current or flow of a stream. In *Turner v. James Canal Co.* (1909) the California Supreme Court ruled that it did not matter if the water in Fresno slough flowed north sometimes and south at other times. Even though streams do not normally act in this manner, the court felt the slough should be considered the same as any other water course.

Another legal concern has been the regularity or the amount of flow. In Texas, Barilla Creek typically flows less than twenty times each year depending on the number of rains. There is water in the creek only a few days after each rain. The bank is three to fifteen feet deep, and the bed is forty to one hundred feet wide. A dam was proposed which could control 350 square miles of the watershed. This would prevent any water from reaching a down-channel land owner. In the lawsuit that followed, the court used a functional rather than a descriptive analysis. Since it was practicable to use the water for irrigation, it was subject to state law (*Hoefs v. Short* 1925). If this same test were used for diffused surface water, its capture would cause it to come under state control.

The interpretation of bed, banks, and flow can be descriptive or functional. If the bed, banks, and flow are obvious, then disputes over whether a stream exists are not likely to occur. Where they are not obvious, courts may use a functional analysis. If the water can be put to a beneficial use, such as irrigation, state law should control its allocation. However, if the water has not yet reached a water course, it may be considered private water.

Pueblo Rights

Most states grant water rights to cities under state law. As a city grows these rights can be expanded by condemning existing rights. Some cities with pueblo water rights can expand their use of water without compensating the person from whom the right was taken. This right, like the right to diffused surface water, is outside the control of the state.

In the Southwest some cities have been recognized as having water rights which date from the time of Spanish or Mexican control (Clark 1960; Gleason 1977; Hoffman 1981a; Hutchins 1960; Kahrl 1982; Kinney 1912; Ostrom 1953). Agricultural villages (pueblos) founded by the Spanish or Mexican government are different from other cities in the United States. They were not given a local charter and were subject to the control of the central government. The first of these pueblos was established by the King of Spain with a special ordinance. The Pueblo of Pictic (Pitic) in Sonora, Mexico was given the right to use the water flowing through the town. This water right was granted to all pueblos subsequently founded. Although these pueblos were granted water rights before they were part of the United States, these rights were recognized by the United States in the Treaty of Guadalupe Hidalgo and by the Gadsden Purchase.

The pueblo water right can be enlarged as a city grows in either population or area. If a boundary expansion takes in new water sources these may become subject to the city's control. Although this water right is not a significant issue in most places, the California courts have granted it to Los Angeles and San Diego (*City of San Diego v. Cuyamaca Water Co.* 1930). In Los Angeles the city has a right to all the water in the Los Angeles River and the ground water that is connected to it. As long as the water is used for municipal purposes the right can lay dormant and then be activated when need arises. This has caused conflict between Los Angeles and neighboring cities which has resulted in litigation (*City of Los Angeles v. City of San Fernando* 1975; *City of Los Angeles v. City of Glendale* 1943). Conflicts have also arisen between Los Angeles and individual water users (*City of Los Angeles v. Los Angeles Farming and Milling Co.* 1908; *City of Los Angeles v. Hunter* 1909; *City of Los Angeles v. Pomoroy* 1899; *Vernon Irrigation Co. v. City of Los Angeles* 1895; *Feliz v. City of Los Angeles* 1881; *City of Los Angeles v. Baldwin* 1879).

The only case outside of California that grants pueblo water rights is *Cartwright v. Public Service Co. of New Mexico* (1958). This New Mexico decision granted Las Vegas, New Mexico, a priority in the use of the Gallinas River. It was awarded a right to as much water as needed for municipal purposes. Several other New Mexico cases mention pueblo rights, but no others have been recognized (*Albuquerque v. Reynolds* 1963; *New Mexico Products Co. v. New Mexico Power Co.* 1937; *State v. Tularosa Community Ditch* 1914).

State Rights

Water is a renewable resource. Thus a state allocation system controls the right to take it and use it over a period of time (Trelease 1979). Water use is controlled by laws which have been developed to encourage desirable human activities and hinder undesirable conduct. Since each state has had the power to regulate water use and create water rights, fifty different state water laws have evolved (Figure 10). Similar physical conditions in the West resulted in the evolution of laws based on a common principle — first in time, first in right. In the East, the English common law riparian rights system was adopted. In a few states both doctrines are used. Differences between state's systems may be blurring with time, however, as many systems have similar aspects (Meyers and Tarlock 1980:196).

The Appropriation Doctrine

Prior to 1850 there was no appropriation doctrine in the United States. Water law was based on the inherited common laws of England. Water rights were recognized in those who owned land adjacent to a river (riparian rights) or lake (littoral rights). Water could be used on adjacent land but not elsewhere. This doctrine worked in the East but was unsuited for conditions in the West; here mineral development provided the need and opportunity for change.

The discovery of gold in 1848 set off a migration which increased California's population from two or three thousand to two or three hundred thousand in a few years (McGowen 1956). Gold was the attraction, but there was no system to control its allocation. The miners were, in fact, trespassers on the public domain (Trelease 1971). It was not until 1866 that the United States passed legislation authorizing their activities

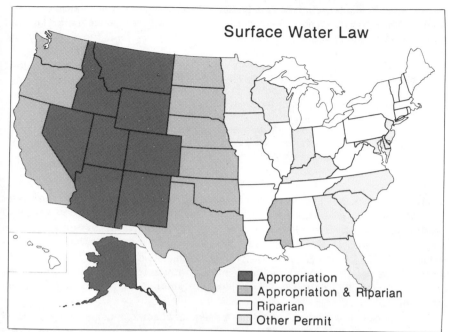

Surface Water Law

Appropriation
Appropriation & Riparian
Riparian
Other Permit

FIGURE 10   CLASSIFICATION OF STATE SURFACE WATER
LAWS (Ausness 1977, 1983; Meyers and Tarlock
1980; Aka. Stats. §46.15.040 1977)

(14 Stat. §§ 251 & 253). As a result the miners themselves had to develop a system that would control resource allocation.

When gold was discovered in an area and the rush to that place began, a mining district would be organized to provide a governing body. Although these bodies varied in complexity, there were certain characteristics common to all. Since much of the districts' function was to prevent conflicts between miners, all developed a set of mining laws. This usually put a limit on the size of each claim, required it to be staked, and provided a register so the claim could be recorded. One of the most important concepts was based on the idea of first in time, first in right. The person who found gold had the right to it above all others, unless the claim was abandoned by failure to work it. This was the basic law adopted by the United States and formed the basis for allocating another essential western resource — water.

The first case accepting the appropriation doctrine was *Irwin v. Phillips* (1855). Water was needed to work the placer deposits first developed in the California gold fields. Some miners had diverted water from a stream to their diggings some distance away. Latecomers staked claims on the streambed and wanted the water returned to its natural channel for their use. The eastern riparian rights doctrine which was commonly accepted at that time would not have allowed the diversion. However, it did not give the latecomers rights either. Since riparian rights exist only in those who own land adjacent to a river, how could a trespasser with no right to the land claim he had a right to the water? The California court decided to depart from traditional common law because it did not seem to fit the circumstances. Its decision followed the same principle as was used in allocating mineral rights — first in time, first in right. The "judge made" law that evolved can be summarized:

> A property right in the use of water is created by diversion of the water from a stream (or lake) and its application to a beneficial use. Water can be used at any location, without regard to the position or place of use in relation to the stream. In the event of a shortage of supply, water will be supplied up to a limit of the right in order of temporal priority; the last man to divert and make use of the stream is the first to have his supply cut off (Meyers 1971:4; footnotes omitted).

Since the first judicial decision a slow evolutionary process has taken place with a combination of statutes and court decisions controlling the allocation of western water rights. In order to get a water right under the common law appropriation system a person must: (1) intend to appropriate the water; (2) divert it from its channel; and (3) apply it to a beneficial use. To these common law elements most states have added the requirement of a permit. Since a permit application shows 'intent to divert,' this has replaced the need to show 'intent' in establishing new water rights. However, the concept is still of importance in establishing priorities that predate the permit requirement.

The cases concerned with intent have risen out of some peculiar circumstances. The water from Abo Wash, New Mexico, naturally irrigated grass in the area. Cows grazed on the grass and some farmers cut hay. Did the farmers intend to appropriate the water by cutting hay and turning stock loose? A New Mexico court held they did not (Reynolds v. Miranda 1972). Often the concept of intent is connected with the idea of 'notice.' Since intent is a frame of mind, courts look to see if there was any open physical act which would show what that intent was. This act should be enough to put others on notice that a water right has been established so time and money are not spent by latecomers (Elk-Rifle Water Co. v. Templeton 1971).

The second requirement for an appropriation is the diversion of water from its natural channel. Specific cases include natural overflow situations and instances where animals have been drinking the water. Both of these situations also create 'intent' problems. In Utah, making use of natural overflow is not an appropriation of water (Hardy v. Beaver County Irrigation Co. 1924), but in Oregon it is (In re Water Rights in Silvies River 1925). Stockwatering appropriations have been frequently upheld (England v. Ally Ong Hing 1969; Stevenson v. Steele 1969; Hunter v. United States 1967; Steptoe Livestock Co. v. Gulley 1931). In Utah, livestock have a right to drink, but no water right is obtained (Adams v. Portage Irrigation Reservoir Power Co. 1937).

The diversion requirement may not always be needed today. Part of its purpose was to give notice to others that a water right existed. Today's permit systems do that. Also, requiring a diversion precludes appropriations for instream uses. To get around this problem states have passed special statutes (Colo. Rev. Stat. § 37-92-102, 1982 supp.). The Idaho Supreme Court upheld (State Dept. of Parks v. Idaho Dept. of Water Administration 1974) a state statute (I.C. § 67-4307, 1980) that directed the Department of Parks to appropriate all of the unappropriated water in designated springs for instream uses.

The water must also be applied to a 'beneficial use.' Mining, manufacturing, irrigation, stock watering and domestic uses have always been considered beneficial uses, but historically recreation and scenic beauty have been more questionable. The early cases were not very charitable (*Empire Water and Power Co. v. Cascade Town Co.* 1913). In Idaho, recreation and scenery are beneficial if the state is doing the appropriation (*State Dept. of Parks v. Idaho Dept. of Water Administration* 1974). In 1973 Colorado passed a statute that allows the appropriation of minimum stream flows to preserve the natural environment (Colo. Rev. Stat. § 37-92,102, 1982 supp.). Although 'beneficial use' was seldom defined in the past, recent statutory changes are including recreation, aesthetics, and preservation of environmental values (Calif. Ann. Code, Water, § 1243, 1971; Mont. Rev. Code § 95-2-102, 1983; N.D. Cent. Code § 61-04-01.1, 1983 supp; Wash. Rev. Code Ann. § 90-54.020(1), 1983 supp.).

In all the appropriation states except Colorado a permit is required to initiate new surface water rights (Meyers and Tarlock 1980). The permit shows the intent to appropriate water and puts others on notice that water is to be used. Permits will be denied in some states if they are not in the public interest (Alaska Stat. § 46.15.080, 1977 supp.; Cal. Ann. Code, Water § 1255, 1971; N.M. Stat. Ann. § 72-5-8, 1978; Ut. Code Ann. § 73-3-8, 1980). In others an environmental impact statement may be required (Wash. Rev. Code Ann. § 43.21C.035, 1983) or costs and benefits considered before a permit will be issued (Wash. Rev. Code Ann. § 90.54.020 (2), 1983 supp.).

The traditional philosophy with regard to water is ably stated in the novel *Centennial* (Michener 1974:568). The goal of the farmers was to see that the South Platte River left the state dry. This attitude is reflected in the Idaho Constitution (Art 15, sec. 3), which states, "The right to divert and appropriate the unappropriated waters of any natural stream to beneficial uses shall never be denied. . . ." Colorado has a similar provision (Colo. Const. Art XVI, sec. 6). Even with this provision there are some grounds for denial in Idaho, including inadequate water supply, interference with another's rights, bad faith, insufficient funds to complete the project, and conflict with local public interest (I.C. § 42-203, 1983 supp.).

The principle which states that priority in time gives priority in right allows early appropriators who are not getting their full amount of water to shut off later appropriators in inverse order of priority until their water right is satisfied (I.C. § 42-106, 1977; Ut. Code Ann. § 73-3-21, 1980). This may create inefficient results. In parts of the mountain West, ranches were established on the valley floors with later ones going progressively up the side canyons. This means the highest priority rights are the furthest downstream. In order for the downstream ranchers to get the full appropriation to which they are entitled, the upstream users may have to allow the stream water to pass by. This is justified because the first ranchers in the valley spent time, money, and effort in building diversion works and developing ranches. If anyone who came along at a later time could destroy the value of this by taking the water from further upstream, why would a downstream appropriator bother to spend money in the first place?

Under the traditional system, the priority date 'related back' to the date of the first 'open step' representing the commencement of labor on the diversion works, as long as the work proceeded with 'due diligence.' This doctrine of 'relation back' was to encourage major works which would take time to construct. If five years' construction work were necessary before water could be diverted, others could have taken it in the interim. There has been some question about when the first 'open step' which gave notice of intent to appropriate was taken (*Colorado River Water Conservancy District v. Twin Lakes Reservoir and Canal Co.* 1973; *Four Counties Water Users Association v.*

Colorado River Water Conservancy District 1966; *City and County of Denver v. Northern Colorado Water Conservancy District* 1954). Today the permit application is considered the first step and priority dates from then. Due diligence is controlled by statute with time limits for beginning and completing work (Ariz. Rev. Stat. § 45-150, 1983 supp.; Idaho Code § 42-217-204, 1983 supp.; Neb. Rev. Stat. § 46-238, 1978; Nev. Rev. Stat. § 533.390, 1981; N. Mex. Comp. L. § 75-5-8, 1978; S. Dak. Comp. Laws § 46-5-25, 1982 supp.; Wyo. Stat. § 41-4-506, 1977).

The senior appropriator has obligations as well as rights. He is protected by his priority date, but others junior to him are protected by a right to have the continuation of the stream conditions as they existed at the time of their appropriations. Changes in point of diversion, place of use or nature of use could materially injure or adversely affect junior appropriators. Since the same water may be used and reused by several persons, all may have rights that entitle them to receive the same molecules of water. If the sale, change in use, or transfer of water makes those molecules unavailable to another, the first user has destroyed the latter's water right. This makes it difficult to treat water as a disposable property right in some western states. Each state treats the changes allowed to a senior in the use of his water rights differently. In some states it is relatively easy, but in others it is very difficult (Ariz. Rev. Stat. Ann. § 45-172, 1983 supp.; I.C. § 42-108, 1977; Ut. Code Ann. § 73-3-3, 1980).

Another early principle of the appropriation doctrine requires continued used of the water, or else the right is lost. Abandonment of a water right requires the cessation of use plus a 'manifestation of intent' to give up the right. This 'manifestation of intent' could be an act which made it obvious that the right was being abandoned. A formal announcement would be enough as would the destruction of all the workings needed to obtain water. It is often difficult to determine if there is 'intent' to abandon. In one case fifty-four years of non-use was inferred to be enough to show intent *(C.F. & I. Steel Corp. v. Purgatory R. Water Cons. Dist.* 1973). There are many cases on this *(Parsons v. Ft. Morgan Res. & Irr. Co.* 1913; *Featherman v. Hennessy* 1911; *Brockman v. Grand Canal Co.* 1904). Because abandonment has been difficult to prove, many states have passed forfeiture statutes which cause an involuntary termination of a water right after a specified period of non-use (I.C. § 42-222(2), 1977). Although forfeiture and abandonment are sometimes used interchangeably, forfeiture results from statute and the intent of the party is unimportant.

Until permits were required, the only secure way to establish a water right was by court order. This may have resolved disputes between the parties to the litigation, but it left the rights of others on a river system unresolved. The western states have been going through an adjudication process in an attempt to quantify all individual rights on different stream systems (Colo. Rev. Stat. § 37-92-101, 1973). In an adjudication all the conflicting water rights in a water shed are quantified and priority dates assigned. This is a slow process, but necessary. Not only are the water rights of individuals involved, but those of irrigation districts and the federal government as well.

This has been an oversimplified description of the appropriation doctrine. The role of irrigation districts and federal reclamation projects has been left out. Enough has been presented so that the complex litigation and statutes that have evolved can be appreciated. Societal responses to conflicts over a scarce resource vary according to circumstances. Since each state had the power to make allocation decisions, different sets of controls evolved among the states. In the West, laws were a response to aridity and scarcity, but conditions in the East were different.

Riparian Rights

When the United States was settled, English water law was in its early stages of development. Uses of water were limited to domestic consumption, powering grist mills, agriculture, fishing, and navigation. The early cases concerned with the use of water recognized that land adjacent to water carried a right to use the water. The question was — what legal standard would allow the greatest beneficial use of the rivers and lakes?

The onset of industrialization created a demand for power generation and waste disposal. To meet this need, industries were located adjacent to rivers. Their activities interfered with the flow, however, which soon created problems. Increased conflicts resulted in court decisions establishing the principle that each riparian landowner has a right to use a river as it passes his property. However, there is no right to injure another riparian landowner. Thus only minor changes to a river were permissible. This principle is called the 'natural flow theory.'

As industralization increased so did the need to consume water. Steam powered generators allowed mills to move from stream banks and consumptive needs increased. New lands were developed requiring irrigation. The doctrine that left a river substantially unchanged became inappropriate. The result was a split in the common law riparian rights. A number of states created the 'reasonable use theory,' while in others the older, 'natural flow theory' prevailed (Hanks 1968).

Under the natural flow theory, a riparian owner has an obligation to leave unimpaired the quantity and quality of the water flowing by his land. The water can be used by the riparian owner as long as he does not materially change it. All riparian land owners have an equal right to the river, and the exercise of this right may not infringe upon the rights of others on the stream. Although this may have been a good doctrine when the same amount of water was needed to be passed from mill to mill for power, it prevents many beneficial uses and is not always strictly enforced *(Mason v. Hoyle* 1888).

Under the reasonable use theory, each riparian landowner has a right to the reasonable use of the water and can prevent unreasonable uses by others. If the use has economic and social value and does not materially harm others, it may be allowed. The problem with a standard based on reasonableness is the inability to predict the uses that will be allowed in a particular situation. One hundred years ago it was acceptable to dump untreated pollutants into rivers. Today that is not necessarily reasonable because 'reasonableness' changes as society's values change. In addition, a use of water on one river may not be acceptable on another because of the characteristics of the river or because of the type of harm that occurs to other riparian owners. On the other hand, a landowner could begin a new use of water which harms his neighbor if the new use provides great benefit against only moderate harm. For example, in an arid area or in time of drought, it may be reasonable to dry up a river.

Although these two riparian rights theories have been discussed as if they are well separated, many court cases in fact mix them. The same court may use both, choosing the theory to meet the facts of the case. Water law in the East, South, and Midwest is not a matter of common law alone; legislation has been passed with many states adopting a permit system. Also, because municipalities did not fit into the riparian system very well, they were granted special power to obtain water.

Which land has riparian rights? One rule states that water may not be taken outside the watershed in the riparian rights system (Farnham 1972). This has created considerable concern recently in eastern areas with water shortages (Abrams 1983). If water from a stream is taken outside the watershed, it is lost to the downstream riparian owners. Such a diversion may be rational, if common property rights exist only in riparian owners. If common property rights in a river belong to 'all' the people, it does not.

Another rule states that the water must be used on adjacent land. There are four theories that have been used to explain which land is adjacent. The 'government survey' rule limits riparian rights to the original government grant adjacent to the river (*Crawford v. Hathway* 1903). The only reason for this is to remain consistent with the federal practice of limiting the amount of land granted an individual. Otherwise the doctrine seems arbitrary (Farnharm 1972).

In the 'smallest tract' rule, the smallest parcel of land adjacent to the river in the history of the title has rights. If a landowner sells land away from the river, that land loses its riparian rights. The rights remain only with the parcel adjacent to the stream. This means that riparian rights apply to a continually decreasing amount of land and can never be increased (*Boehmer v. Big Rock Irr. Dist.* 1897).

The 'no limit' rule is the opposite of the smallest tract rule, putting no limit on the size of a tract of land. If a riparian land owner buys adjacent land the new common unit has riparian rights. This allows the amount of land with riparian rights to be expanded. Increasing the amount of land with water rights might interfere with other established rights since more water could be consumed than before. However, this theory is well accepted in the United States (*Jones v. Conn.* 1901).

The 'reasonable limit' rule suggested by Farnham (1972) would allow the expansion of riparian land as in the no limit rule, but would contain it to land within a reasonable distance of the river. This reasonable distance limitation would protect other riparian owners, with the extent of the protection depending upon the interpretation of 'reasonable.'

Today, both the appropriation and riparian rights systems have been modified by permits. However, they still remain distinct with the following major differences (Beuscher 1961:449; modified):

1. The right is attached to adjacent land in the riparian system and in the appropriation system it is given to someone who diverts water and applies it to a beneficial use.

2. Non-use will destroy the right in the appropriation system, but a riparian owner does not lose it and can establish new uses.

3. Riparians use the water on contiguous land within the watershed, but appropriators may use the water anywhere.

4. Riparians share in the reasonable use of water with no fixed quantity assured them. An appropriator has a right to a specific quantity subject to the priority date.

5. In time of shortage all suffer equally in the riparian system, but in an appropriation state priorities control water allocation.

These differences are blurring with the addition of a priority concept to the approval of permits in some eastern states and the distinctive way cities are treated under both systems.

Federal Rights

Although state water law has major responsibility for the allocation of water rights, federal law must also be considered, as the power of the federal government to control the use of water under the constitution is extensive. For example, constitutionally granted federal rights are superior to state rights.

Constitutional Power

The parts of the constitution that can be used to control water include: the treaty power, the war power, admiralty jurisdiction, the general welfare clause, the property clause and the commerce clause (Leighty 1970). Federal power under these provisions is often stated in terms of power over navigable waters with different definitions for navigability.

The treaty power *(Oklahoma v. Texas* 1922) and the war power are seldom used for controlling water use, but the potential is there. In the past, admiralty jurisdiction cases have involved personal injury and other tort liabilities, but this jurisdiction could be used to extend control over recreational boating (White 1958a; Note 1968, 1978). The general welfare clause has been used in association with reclamation projects allowing federal programs to prevail over conflicting state ones *(Ivanhoe Irrigation Dist. v. McCracken* 1958). The property clause creates the power to control federal lands.

The most important of these clauses is the commerce clause. In 1824 Chief Justice John Marshall of the United States Supreme Court held that commerce included transportation and that commercial navigation was part of transportation *(Gibbons v. Ogden).* The traditional definition for navigability that has developed under the commerce clause is not the same as the one used to determine bed ownership discussed in Chapter 3 and may no longer be valid after the *Sporhase* case to be discussed below. In ownership cases the water bodies must be "susceptible of being used in their ordinary condition, as highways for commerce . . ." *(The Daniel Ball* 1870). Under the commerce clause a water body is navigable if it can be made so by reasonable improvements. Improvements do not actually have to be made or even authorized; it is enough that they are possible. The determination of 'reasonable improvements' is not fixed at some past date, but may be made at some future time so that places not now navigable may become so in the future *(United States v. Appalachian Elec. Power Co.* 1940).

Also, the water body must form a 'highway for interstate commerce.' It is not enough that it is navigable only within the boundaires of one state, although that would be sufficient for bed ownership under the federal test. Under the commerce clause the water body does not have to be used for commerce, it need only have an 'effect' on 'interstate' commerce. This means that non-navigable tributaries of navigable rivers can be regulated because they "affect" navigable streams *(Oklahoma ex. rel. Phillips v. Guy F. Atkinson Co.* 1941; *United States v. Rio Grande Dam & Irr. Co.* 1899).

It is possible for a landlocked water body to be navigable under the federal test for bed ownership purposes but not under the commerce clause. In ownership cases 'navigation' must have actually occurred at some time (Davies 1978a), but if no state line had been crossed it might not be 'interstate' commerce. This happened with the Great Salt Lake *(Utah v. United States* 1971; *Hardy Salt Co. v. Southern Pacific Transp. Co.* 1974).

The definition for admiralty jurisdiction is interpreted differently from the one used for bed ownership. Admiralty jurisdiction is not related to any date *(United States v. Appalachian Elec. Power Co.* 1940), while bed ownership tests navigability at statehood. Canals and other artificial water bodies can be navigable for admiralty jurisdiction *(Ex parte Boyer* 1884), but for bed ownership they must be in their "natural and ordinary condition" *(United States v. Holt State Bank* 1926).

Although navigability under the commerce clause and admiralty jurisdiction have been defined similarly by the Supreme Court, in recent legislation Congress has employed an expanded definition of commerce, making its power under the commerce clause seemingly without limit. The Clean Water Act is one of the best examples of the expanded use of the commerce clause. In the act, navigable waters are defined as "the waters of the United States including the territorial seas" (33 U.S.C. § 1362, 1978). Although this may seem vague, it has been upheld by a federal district court *(United States v. Oxford Royal Mushroom Products Inc.* 1980) and is given the broadest meaning possible in the seventh circuit *(United States v. Byrd* 1979). There is still no United States Supreme Court opinion on this. The present definition of waters of the United States derived from this act includes:

> *(a) All waters which are currently used, were used in the past, or may be susceptible to use in interstate or foreign commerce, including all waters which are subject to the ebb and flow of the tide;*
> *(b) All interstate waters, including interstate "wetlands";*
> *(c) All other waters such as intrastate lakes, rivers, streams (including intermittent streams), mudflats, sandflats, "wetlands," sloughs, prairie potholes, wet meadows, playa lakes, or natural ponds the use, degradation, or destruction of which would affect or could affect interstate or foreign commerce including any such waters:*
> > *(1) Which are or could be used by interstate or foreign travelers for recreational or other purposes;*
> > *(2) From which fish or shellfish are or could be taken and sold in interstate or foreign commerce; or*
> > *(3) Which are used or could be used for industrial purposes by industries in interstate commerce.*
> *(d) All impoundments of waters otherwise defined as waters of the United States under this definition;*
> *(e) Tributaries of waters identified in paragraphs (a)-(d) of this definition;*
> *(f) The territorial sea; and*
> *(g) "Wetlands" adjacent to waters (other than waters that are themselves wetlands) identified in paragraphs (a) through (f) of this definition.*
> *(40 C.F.R. § 122.4, 1983)*

Legislative history (1972 U.S. Code Cong. and Admin. News 3821) suggests the intent of Congress was to affirm the idea that all water in the United States is navigable. Representative Dingle, a supporter of the measure, explained the phrase by saying 'water of the United States' was used in a geographic sense rather than in the sense of the technical legal definitions often associated with the term 'navigable water' (118 Cong. Rec. 33756, 1976). The evolution of the navigation concept from ocean going navigation represented by the ebb and flow of tides, to all water geographically within the United States, whether it can be 'navigated' or not, represents a significant change. Navigability for purposes of the commerce clause has become a term related to the public's interest in water, with the ability of a boat to float on it becoming less important. Not all federal legislation extends the commerce clause concept of navigation as far as the Clean Water Act, however. Since acts of Congress are designed to accomplish specific purposes, they all need not be as expansive. In 1890 Congress passed an act pursuant to the commerce clause which prohibited obstructions to the "navigable capacity" of waters within the United States (26 Stat. 454). The Rivers and Harbors Act of 1899 (33 U.S.C. § 407, 1970) made it unlawful to discharge refuse into navigable waters. Under the Federal Power Act of 1920 (16 U.S.C. § 791a, 1974) the Federal Power Commission was authorized to issue licenses for almost all projects that had material effects on stream flow. Flood control activities may also be regulated (33 U.S.C. § 701, 1970).

Federal power under the commerce clause has been summarized as follows:

The power to control navigation and navigable waters includes the power to destroy the navigable capacity of the waters and prevent navigation by the construction of obstructions. It also includes the power to protect the navigable capacity by preventing diversions of the water itself, or of the non-navigable tributaries that affect navigability, or by preventing obstructions by bridges or dams or by constructing flood control structures on the navigable waters or on their non-navigable tributaries or even on the watersheds of the rivers and tributaries. The powers to prevent obstruction in turn lead to powers to license obstructions. The power to obstruct leads to the power to generate electric energy from the dammed water (Trelease 1961:400, footnotes omitted).

A more recent statement by the Supreme Court includes groundwater as an article of commerce *(Sporhase v. Nebrakska* 1982). Since legislation passed under the constitutional authority of the commerce clause prevails over conflicting state law, the federal definition of navigable water will have a considerable impact on resource use. This can be demonstrated by the following example.

In 1949 the state of Washington passed an act prohibiting the construction of dams over 25 feet high on some of the tributaries of the Columbia River. The statute was enacted to protect anadromous fish. The city of Tacoma wanted to build dams 510 and 240 feet high on the Cowlitz River, which was one of the regulated tributaries. It applied for a license from the Federal Power Commission who granted it after a 'finding of need.' The state objected because it wanted to leave the river in its natural condition. The authority of the Federal Power Commission to issue the license was challenged, but the state lost because federal power is supreme when dealing with electric power *(City of Tacoma v. Taxpayers of Tacoma* 1953).

This did not end the dispute, because there was a state fish hatchery on the river. A Washington court ruled in *City of Tacoma v. Taxpayers of Tacoma* (1957) that the city of Tacoma did not have the power to condemn the hatchery in order to construct the dams. The hatchery was on the river and would be destroyed by the completion of the project. The United States Supreme Court *(City of Tacoma v. Taxpayers of Tacoma* 1958) reversed the decision, ruling that state law could not prevent the one who received the license from building the dam. In response the people of Washington passed an initiative in 1960 that would have prevented construction. This was overturned by the Washington Supreme Court again, because of federal supremacy *(City of Tacoma v. Taxpayers of Tacoma* 1962).

This demonstrates that federal authority under the commerce clause is 'supreme' in controlling navigable waters. It also shows that the goals of one segment of society may be overridden by national policy. The city, in following federal policy under the Federal Power Act, was able to suppress the wishes of the people of the state after the federal license was issued.

Types of Federal Rights

There are several types of water rights exercised by the federal government (Trelease 1978). Inherent rights result from the exercise of constitutional power, as discussed above. Also, the federal government has rights established under state law. If the federal government acquires a piece of land, rights that were attached to the land pursuant to state law persist in becoming what is known as 'federal acquired rights.' The government may also apply for an appropriation permit under state law, even though it may not be needed (County of Trinity v. Andrus 1977). Furthermore, there are reserved water rights outside the state allocation system on federal lands.

The federal government retained ownership over public land until it was granted to individuals under authority of the property clause. At times land was withdrawn from agricultural or mineral entry and set aside for some special purpose. National parks, national forests, and Indian reservations fit this category. A body of special federal water rights developed for this type of land. In 1908 the United States Supreme Court recognized that a group of Montana Indians had a water right with a priority over those granted under state law (Winters v. United States 1908). This became known as the 'Winters,' or 'reserved rights,' doctrine. When the government withdraws part of its land from the public domain, it simultaneously reserves a water right which is large enough to accomplish the purposes of the reservation.

Only unappropriated water can be reserved, and rights already established under state law have priority. But the federal right is not recorded, not fixed to a specific amount, and need not be a 'beneficial purpose' for state law. A priority date attaches to the water right at the time the reservation is made. Water rights for Indian lands may thus have an early priority, since many reservations were established before non-Indian settlement. The right is not subject to state law on abandonment and cannot be lost through non-use. If the purpose of the reservation expands, it may be possible that the accompanying reserved water right would expand also. In this case the added portion of the right might have a later priority, dating from the time of expansion.

A major Supreme Court decision (Arizona v. California 1963) started a flurry of litigation which has begun to define the limits of this doctrine. In that case an Indian reservation was held to own the rights to enough water to serve all of their irrigable land. United States v. Cappaert (1976) centered on water in a pool that was the home of the devil's hole pupfish. Pumping of ground water was draining the pool. The area was a national monument which had been set aside, in part, for the preservation of the pupfish. To 'accomplish this purpose' the federal government had reserved a water right — enough ground water had been reserved to keep the pool level at a sufficient height to allow pupfish breeding. Any use, however lawful under state law, that interfered with the federal right was declared subservient to it.

For a period of time in the 1970s it looked as if the federal reserved water right might completely swallow state water law. One attempt was made to exercise a water right on national forest land for minimum stream flows, and scenic and recreational uses. The Creative Act of 1891 (26 Stat. 1095 & 1103) and Organic Administration Act of 1897 (16 U.S.C. § 471, 1974) were being relied upon to show that Congress intended the national forests for such purposes when they were set aside. However, the Supreme Court decided (*United States v. New Mexico* 1978) that the intent of these acts was merely to grow trees and protect the watershed. Since there was no early intent for other purposes, the amount of water claimed under this doctrine was deemed much less than was asserted.

The major reserved rights remaining are those attached to Indian lands. Reservations were established in order to 'civilize' the Indians (*Winters v. U.S.* 1908). What this policy means and how it determines the extent of the water right that goes with the reservation has been subject to considerable litigation. It would seem that if the purpose of the reservation is 'civilization,' the water right should expand and change as the needs of Indian communities change. In 1963 *Arizona v. California* held that Indian reservations had water rights to all 'practicably' irrigable acreage.

When *Arizona v. California* was decided the boundaries of some of the Indian reservations involved in the dispute were not clear. When title to the disputed acreage was finally resolved by a state court, the Supreme Court held (*Arizona v. California* 1983) that water rights existed on the irrigable acreage of these lands also. The Court said, however, that as to the original undisputed acreage, the determination of water rights in 1963 was final and would not be relitigated. This limits the open-ended expandability of Indian water rights. The message is the same in *Nevada v. United States* (1983), where the right to additional water for the Pyramid Lake fishery was denied because the rights had been adjudicated in 1944. Since state courts have the power to resolve Indian rights, and since this determination will be binding, the future needs of 'civilization' may not be considered (*Arizona v. San Carlos Apache Tribe of Arizona* 1983).

The Limit on Federal Rights

The movement of goods across state boundaries within the United States is generally unimpaired. This was not always true. When the Revolutionary War ended, commercial warfare between the states emerged. Economic barriers disrupted trade, and the need for centralized control over commerce was realized. The decision was made that the country must operate as a single economc unit rather than each state having separate control. It was recognized that if each state could regulate commerce entering or leaving its borders, thirteen different sets of laws could create economic chaos (*Hood & Sons v. Dumond* 1949).

The mechanism created to settle this imbroglio was the commerce clause of the Constitution, which grants Congress legislative power over commerce. The clause has been interpreted to be a prohibition on state laws that discriminate against or burden interstate commerce (Tarlock 1983a). The two parts of the commerce clause erase the impact of internal boundaries on trade and create a common national economic policy.

How does federal power over commerce control the distribution of water? Originally the federal government was not involved in controlling water except for navigation purposes, and the states were allowed to develop their own allocation systems. Recently, there has been an increasing federal interest. The limitations on federal power was discussed by the United States Supreme Court in 1982. Although the case was related to groundwater, it also affects surface water.

In 1982 Nebraska had a statute that required a permit be issued before groundwater could be exported. The permit was to be issued if the request "is reasonable, is not contrary to the conservation and use of ground water, and is not otherwise detrimental to public welfare . . ." (Neb. Rev. Stat. § 46-613.01, 1978). However, the permit would not be issued unless the state in which the water was to be used granted reciprocal rights. This would have prevented the movement of water between Colorado and Nebraska.

Joy Sporhase and Delmar Moss jointly owned contiguous tracts of farm land in Nebraska and Colorado. Their well was located in Nebraska and their land in Colorado was irrigated from it. Since they had no Nebraska permit to export water, the state of Nebraska tried to enjoin their out-of-state activities. In the court action that followed, the Nebraska Supreme Court ruled that water was not freely transferable within the state and was therefore not an item of commerce (*State v. Sporhase* 1981). For this reason Nebraska had the authority to deny the exportation of water.

On appeal, the United States Supreme Court (*Sporhase v. Nebraska* 1982) sought to decide three issues: (1) Is water an article of commerce? (2) If so, does the Nebraska statute impose an impermissible burden on commerce? (3) Has Congress granted the states an otherwise impermissible right to regulate?

In addressing whether water was an article of commerce, the court considered two contradictory precedents. In 1908 the Supreme Court upheld a New Jersey statute that prevented water from being exported (*Hudson Co. Water Co. v. McCarter*). Many issues were involved in that case, but only three sentences addressed the commerce clause. The other precedent was a three-judge federal district court (*City of Altus v. Carr* 1966) which found a Texas export ban of water an impermissible burden on interstate commerce. The United States Supreme Court had affirmed this without making a written decision. Resolving these opinions the Supreme Court in *Sporhase* said:

> But appellee's claim that Nebraska groundwater is not an article of commerce goes too far; it would not only exempt Nebraska ground water regulation from burden-on-commerce analysis, it also would curtail the affirmative power of Congress to implement its own policies concerning such regulation. If Congress chooses to legislate in this area under its commerce power, its regulation need not be more limited in Nebraska than in Texas and states with similar property laws. Ground water overdraft is a national problem and Congress has the power to deal with it on that scale (346; citations omitted).

This means water is an article of commerce and Congress has the power to supersede state water law if it chooses. Whether that power is ever asserted at the federal level is a political question.

Holding that water is an item of commerce, the Court next had to determine whether the Nebraska statute was an impermissible burden on commerce. State statutes are permitted to affect commerce: (1) if a legitimate local purpose is found and the burden on commerce is not excessive when compared to the local benefits; and (2) if there are no alternatives with a lesser impact (*Pike v. Bruce Church, Inc.* 1970).

One local purpose stated by Nebraska was to preserve and conserve diminishing groundwater sources. The court found this to be a legitimate purpose, especially since people within the state were being restricted in the way water was used. However, the court could not find any evidence that the reciprocity provision was tailored to the goal of conservation and preservation. In an interesting bit of dictum, the court left the door open for possible future bans. It said: "[a] demonstrably arid state conceivably might be able to marshall evidence to establish a close means-end relationship between even a total ban on the exportation of water and a purpose to conserve and preserve water" (3465). Since the statute did not satisfy the first condition, the court did not need to examine whether there were alternatives with a lesser impact.

The third issue before the Court was important because Congress can grant the states the power to enact legislation that would otherwise be impermissible under the constitution. Nebraska argued that the thirty-seven federal statutes that defer to state water law did this. Most of these statutes state that nothing in them is intended to interfere with state water laws and that federal agencies must act in conformity with those laws. The Court did not agree with this argument, deciding that the grant of power to a state must be expressly stated in a statute in order to affect interstate commerce.

In rejecting Nebraska's statute, the Court set standards under which other state statutes could be judged. In January 1983 those standards were interpreted by a federal district judge in New Mexico.

Currently El Paso, Texas, obtains its water supply from within the state. Since these supplies will be insufficient in the future, El Paso sought to obtain groundwater from neighboring New Mexico. The city applied for 326 permits to appropriate 296,000 acre-feet of water, but the permits were denied — New Mexico statutes prohibited the exportation of groundwater (except for one inconsequential provision; N.M. Stat. Ann. § 72-12-19, 1978). El Paso sought an injunction to prohibit the ban (*El Paso v. Reynolds* 1983). While most of the resultant court decision addressed unrelated jurisdictional issues, the commerce clause was also discussed.

An absolute ban on exporting water is a basically discriminatory statute and is subject to the strictest scrutiny under the commerce clause. This is a stricter standard than was applied in the *Sporhase* case because the New Mexico statute prohibits all exports. Applying this standard to the New Mexico statute the district court ruled that New Mexico "must demonstrate that the embargo serves a legitimate local purpose, that it is narrowly tailored to that purpose, and that there are no adequate non-discriminatory alternatives" (388).

New Mexico maintained that the purpose of the export ban was to conserve and preserve the state's water. The court thought this was a legitimate purpose under the three pronged test in the preceding paragraph, but it was not enough to support a discriminatory total ban. Interpreting *Sporhase* the court said:

> [A] state may discriminate in favor of its citizens only to the extent that water is essential to human survival. Outside of fulfilling human survival needs water is an economic resource. For purposes of constitutional analysis under the Commerce Clause, it is to be treated the same as any other natural resources (389).

The court determined that New Mexico had no shortage of water for health or safety reasons and would not in the near future. The need for water for irrigated agriculture and energy production was said to be a matter of economics, not health and safety.

The court characterized New Mexico policy as being "tantamount to economic protectionism." Keeping water for economic development in New Mexico while denying it for economic development outside the state is discriminatory and goes against the principle that the county has a single nationwide economic unit — not 50 states. This does not mean that New Mexico cannot conserve or preserve water — only that interstate and intrastate uses must be treated equally, unless there is a threat to health and safety.

The court also rejected the New Mexico statute under the second test, because it was not "narrowly tailored" to achieve the local purpose. The statute did not restrict any in-state uses of water. Indeed, permits were not denied if there was unappropriated water. When this is added to the fact there were alternate ways to accomplish the state's purposes, the court concluded the ban was unconstitutional.

In interpreting the commerce clause and its application to water exportation, a two level analysis is needed (Tarlock 1983a). If a statute basically discriminates against interstate commerce or citizens of another state, then it will be strictly scrutinized. An example of this is the absolute prohibition. In order for this type of statute to be constitutional it must: (1) serve a local purpose related to public health and safety; (2) be narrowly tailored to that purpose; and (3) have no nondiscriminatory alternatives available. This is a difficult standard, and it is doubtful that many anti-export statutes could meet it.

If the statute is not basically discriminatory then another test is used. In this test there needs to be: (1) a legitimate local purpose; (2) benefits outweighing the burden imposed on commerce; and (3) no alternatives with a lesser impact on commerce. This creates a balancing test in which burdens and benefits are weighed. Clearly this test is easier to meet than the one used for basically discriminatory statutes.

There are still possibilities for state control of water exportation. The first step is to treat all appropriators the same whether they are from inside or outside the state. This eliminates basically discriminatory statutes. The statute must have a legitimate local purpose, like water conservation. In areas where demand exceeds supply there will be more room for restrictions than where there is a surplus of water. Draw-down restrictions, well spacing, pumping rates, and anti-mining statutes could be justified where water is limited. A comprehensive conservation plan which uses a variety of devices is most likely to succeed, since alternatives with lesser impacts on commerce will not be excluded.

There is another way states may be able to control their water. Congress can authorize a state to pass a statute which would otherwise impermissibly burden interstate commerce. At present there are several bills in Congress which may have some impact. These bills are aimed at granting coal slurry pipeline companies the power of eminent domain so they can condemn a right of way. One bill would allow otherwise impermissible state restraints on interstate commerce. Others would allow for a free market environment or consider only the exportation of water for coal.

Legislation on this issue could remove it from the judicial arena. Otherwise, courts will continue to make the decisions. It may be that politics, not law, will provide the proper forum for this issue.

5

Boundary Changes

Boundary changes and disputes have long been a central part of political geography, with most of the work being done on international boundaries. The classic work is Stephen B. Jones's *Boundary Making* (1945) which contains two chapters on international water boundaries. Similar issues may be raised when a river forms the boundary between two political subdivisions within a country. The typical dispute under international law requires determination of the midpoint on a river and how it shifts. In state boundary cases the issue is, in addition, where does water end and land begin?

Where is the River's Edge?

The proprietary interests of the bed owner and of the adjacent upland owner control public use of the water's surface and adjacent shoreline. Determining the boundary between them is important. If a state owns the river bed, the public's right to use both it and the overlying water is greater than the public rights that could otherwise be granted over the area under the state's police power. With the latter authority, the state may have formal jurisdiction over the entire area, but its control over the bed with the former includes the power of a property owner.

Even if both the bed and the upland area are privately owned, it may still be important to determine the boundary between them. For example, a federal navigational servitude may extend over private beds. This doctrine gives the federal government the right to control activities on the bed under navigable waters. The same is true for the states' power to regulate water. A law may be passed which applies only to the bed and water above it and not to the upland area. Two factors are important — river boundaries and the changes that occur when rivers alter their channels.

The Extent of the Bed

The description of the boundary of the bed of a water body has evolved through common law and exists at both the federal and state levels. In most instances the ordinary high water line (OHWL) is the boundary, but some states use a low water line (Maloney 1978). This difference in definition may be significant in terms of access along navigable streams. If the water level in a stream fluctuates, the bed below the OHWL may be exposed. This means that the upland owner, if his property ends at the OHWL, will be separated from the stream by a strip of public land during times of low water. The public may be entitled to access over this. If the low water line is used, then a strip of

land will not appear adjacent to the stream, and there may not be any public use
e bank allowed.

The problems in defining the ordinary high water line of streams are different from
se associated with defining the ordinary high water line for tidal waters. Statistical
eraging can be used with tides, but this is not necessarily appropriate when dealing
vith inland waters. Most definitions look at the physical charcteristics at the water's
edge and emphasize visible features. The most common definition comes from the
1851 United States Supreme Court decision *Howard v. Ingersoll*. The case involved a
boundary dispute on the Chattahooche River between Georgia and Alabama. Georgia
had conveyed land west of its current boundaries to the United States at the time the
Union was formed. The document of conveyance described the boundary as the
western bank of the river, but left unexplained what this meant.

The three written opinions in the case do not clarify the definition of the "bank"
completely. The majority said:

> When banks of rivers were spoken of, those boundaries were meant
> which contain their water at the highest flow . . . the line neither takes in
> over-flowed land beyond the bank, nor includes swamps or low grounds
> liable to be overflowed, but reclaimed for meadows or agriculture. . . .
> Such a line may be found upon every river from its source to its mouth. It
> requires no scientific exploration to find or mark it out. The eye traces it in
> going either up or down a river in any stage of water (Howard v. Ingersoll
> 1857:415-416).

There are three concepts in this particular definition. First, the boundary is to be drawn
at the highest flow of the river. Secondly, swamps and low areas are not part of the river,
especially if they are potentially usable by the upland owner. If one can use it, one
should own it. Any other policy would exclude potentially usable land from private use.
The third aspect of the definition is based on the visible nature of the banks which can
be determined by inspecting the river.

A concurring opinion was more restrictive in its definition, stating that the boundary
should be determined by the level of the water at its "usual and accustomed stage"
which can be seen as a line "marked along its borders by the almost constant presence
and abrasion of the water against the bank" *(Howard v. Ingersoll* 1851:424). This
ignored the economic usability concept and emphasized a line visible because of
action by the river. The definition in the third opinion is similar to the second, with the
physical characteristics of the bank again being emphasized. This definition eventually
became the standard:

> This line is to be found by examining the bed and banks, and ascertain-
> ing where the presence and action of water are so common and usual
> and so long continued in all ordinary years as to mark upon the soil of the
> bed a character so distinct from that of the banks, in respect to veg-
> etation, as well as in respect to the nature of the soil itself (427).

The test that evolved emphasized the physical characteristics of soil and vegetation. Sometimes these are stated in terms of suitability for agriculture, but not
always. Although this definition has been standardized, it is not easy to apply to some
situations.

Braided streams are characterized by a multiplicity of channels that are constantly
changing. The examination of vegetation characteristics normally used to determine

the boundary is not useful in this instance. In the *Snake River Ranch v. United State.* (1975) this situation arose, and a federal district court, departing from the traditional definition, held the line was "the outer boundaries of the braided channel that carries water during the substantial part of the snowmelt high-flow period . . ." (893).

In another case a duck hunter was held to have the right to hunt in a marshy area that was covered by water only part of the year *(Diana Shooting Club v. Husting* 1914). Also, there have been problems when large trees continue to grow after their base becomes covered with water *(State v. Sorenson* 1937).

In some instances *(Trustees of Internal Improvement Fund v. Wetstone* 1969) meander lines have been used to establish the ordinary high water mark. These lines are established by public survey and consist of a series of straight lines connecting points along the shore. This was done to determine the exact quantity of a parcel of land to be sold. The meander line is not the true boundary since it is a series of straight line segments used to approximate a curved high water line. If the water line is obscured for some reason then the meander line may be used, since it may be the best evidence of where the ordinary high water mark was. This occurred where the mean high water line was obscured by road fill in *Hawkins v. Alaska Freight Lines Inc.* (1966). Another recent case illustrates how this approach was used.

The land surrounding the Great Salt Lake in Utah is extremely flat. The variable rainfall in the area causes the lake level to fluctuate, exposing or inundating vast areas of land. The bed of the lake belongs to the state and much of the upland area is managed by the Bureau of Land Management. A drop in water level of six feet will expose 396,000 acres of the lake's bed. This presented a management problem of considerable magnitude. In order to establish the boundary between federal and state land a special master was appointed to hear the case; his decision was adopted by the United States Supreme Court *(Utah v. United States* 1971).

The boundary should have been established where the level of the lake was in 1896, when Utah became a state, since the bed of navigable waters becomes state property at that time. But there were two problems in determining what that level had been. An examination of the physical characteristics was inconclusive and could not be used to determine the shoreline since there is little vegetation in the basin and no difference in soil. Also, the area is subject to seismic activity and in 1934 an earthquake tilted the northern part of the basin so that a constant elevation above sea level would not define the boundary of the lake at the time of statehood. Because of these problems the meander line was used as the boundary. Permanently fixing the boundary line is not usually acceptable because accretion and reliction operate to allow the line to change constantly.

Changes in the Boundary

Since change in the size and location of river channels is a natural occurrence, changing channels affect the boundary between the bed and upland owners. There are several terms that describe the processes that occur. These are related to the rate of change and the method by which the change is made (Maloney 1978:493; Comment 1976:321; Note 1972:325).

Accretion: *Soil is deposited in an area that was once under water, thereby creating new land.*

Reliction (dereliction): *Water recedes and new land is exposed.*

Erosion: *Soil is carried away by action of water so that the area becomes covered by water.*

Submergence: *Water covers previously dry land by raising the water level (inundation) or lowering the land level (subsidence).*

Reemergence: *Land that was dry becomes covered with water and then becomes dry again.*

Avulsion: *A change in a water boundary that is not gradual or imperceptible.*

Jones suggested (1945:120):

> *Accretion may be defined as a lateral movement continuous in the space sense. It need not be continuous in the time sense. If the stream shifts bodily, taking a new course without removing piece by piece from its bank, it is said to shift by avulsion. . . . Avulsion may be defined as a lateral movement discontinuous in the space sense. In the time sense, the actual avulsion is almost instantaneous.*

New land area is created by accretion and reliction, and land is lost by erosion and submergence. Accretion and erosion are part of a process involving soil movements. Reliction, submergence and reemergence involve a change in water level in relation to the land.

In general, slow changes that occur through any of these processes mean a shift in the boundary. Thus, a land owner whose property is being slowly eroded will have a constantly decreasing land area. If slow accretion or reliction is occurring, then the landowner owns a constantly increasing area. If the change is rapid (avulsion), then the boundary lines do not shift, and ownership stays as it is. This is the accepted method with international boundaries and has been adopted for the internal boundaries of the United States (*Iowa v. Illinois* 1893; *Nebraska v. Iowa* 1892). Although it is simple to generalize about the legal concept, it is difficult to apply it to specific situations (Beck 1967; Comment 1976; Comment 1977a; Johnannson 1977; Maloney 1978; Note 1972). Two recent court cases will be examined below.

There are several rationale used to justify giving relicted or accreted land to the upland owner (Note 1972). The Roman theory of accession recognizes that the owner of the mother animal owns the offspring and to the tree's owner belongs the fruit. Additions to a river bank are likened to 'offspring.' Another justification stems from the nature of the water boundary. If a river's edge serves as a boundary, it should continue to serve as a boundary. If it were otherwise, the landowner would be cut off from the stream. The English courts adopted a *de minimus* concept and refused to consider small changes.

Today, the best reasons to continue the policy are based on economic or management considerations. The upland owner is in the best position to make productive use of the added land. Since landowners may lose land through erosion, allowing them to gain it back through accretion may compensate for this loss. If ownership is not transferred during accretion or reliction, the riparian character of the upland would be lost. Alternative concepts would entail tracing the migration of specific soil particles and proving ownership.

This is not as simple a concept to apply as it might seem at first. *Bonelli Cattle Co. v. Arizona* (1973) was a significant Supreme Court decision regarding changes in the

Colorado River. In 1910, just north of the Fort Mohave Indian Reservation, one-half of a section of land was patented by the predecessor to the Bonelli Cattle Co., which gained ownership in 1955. Two years after the original patent Arizona became a state. Since the Colorado River is considered navigable, the state got title to the river bed. A United States Geological Survey map made in 1902-3 showed the location of the river as one-quarter mile west of the land in question. By 1938 the river had moved eastward eroding all but 60 acres of the parcel. Since the change was slow the boundary between the upland owner and the state had legally shifted.

After Hoover Dam was in operation in 1938, the river stopped moving eastward. In 1960 a federal dredging project exposed the land Bonelli had lost next to the remaining 60 acres. In 1970 Bonelli went to court and wanted title to it. The Arizona Supreme Court, using state law, held that the land between the 60 acres and the river belonged to the state. The United States Supreme Court disagreed, however, refusing to use the state law as it had in the past. Instead, a different standard was used.

The Arizona court had considered the change an avulsive one since the dredging had caused a sudden change in the character of the land. According to Arizona law, sudden changes do not change ownership. However, the United States Supreme Court decided as a matter of policy that the state should not receive this land. For the state to possess this land was characterized as a windfall to the state and as unnecessary for controlling navigation on the river. Thus, the Court departed from traditional interpretations which related shifts in the boundary to the speed with which the change occurred. In the new standard a public purpose such as navigation could be used in examining changes. This radical departure from past decisions did not last long and was overturned by the United States Supreme Court in *Oregon ex. rel. State Land Board v. Corvallis Sand and Gravel Co.* (1977).

Between 1853 and 1909 Fischer Island had formed a peninsula over which the Willamette River occasionally flowed. By 1890 there was a distinct overflow channel (Fischer cut) across the neck of the peninsula. This channel was full of driftwood and willows, but it carried water at the high and intermediate stages of the river. About one fourth of the flow of the river went through there in 1890. Before 1909 there was some clearing in the channel. In 1909 a violent flood occurred on the river — water swept over the lowland area, making it the main channel.

The state of Oregon, asserting title to the former bed, filed suit in 1959 to stop a gravel company from removing gravel from it and to secure payment of royalties to the state. It took four decisions from the Oregon Supreme Court and one from the United States Supreme Court to resolve the dispute. The United States Supreme Court based its decision on the 'equal footing' doctrine and reversed *Bonelli*. The original thirteen colonies were free to choose their own legal principles in resolving disputes related to river bed ownership. By imposing federal common law requirements on the other states the Court in *Bonelli* had denied them their equal footing. State laws were proper to use in resolving disputes of this nature. The case was sent back to Oregon Courts and Oregon law was used in the final decision.

Some of the parcels were determined to be state land and some private. The bed of Fischer Cut was not considered navigable before 1909 even though some water had been flowing through it. Since the court found the change was sudden, the ownership had not changed and Fischer Cut remained private. The state continued to own those areas it had before the change. For the 660,000 cubic yards of material the gravel company removed, $82,500 in damages were assessed to equal lost state royalties.

The Middle of the River

River boundaries between the states of the United States are frequently described as being the middle of the river. 'Middle' is seldom defined; it or some similar term is used to indicate the river is a shared resource.

On international rivers the same concept exists, and splitting the river was historically based on sharing navigation. Since the bed of a river does not have a uniform depth, the 'middle' of the deepest channel or 'thalweg' may be used as the boundary rather than a line equal distant between the banks. Since the deepest part is not always the normal channel of navigation, exceptions have been made.

Using the thalweg or navigational channel has been introduced into internal disputes in the United States. There seems to be little reason for doing this, because there is an equal right to navigate waters of the United States regardless of which state claims jurisdiction. Sharing the right to tax and fish may still be important, but is drawing a boundary in the deepest part of the river the most equitable way to share these rights?

The United States Supreme Court has endorsed this principle in many cases (*Arkansas v. Tennessee* 1940; *Wisconsin v. Michigan* 1935; *New Jersey v. Delaware* 1934; *Minnesota v. Wisconsin* 1919; *Arkansas v. Tennessee* 1918). In most of these cases the Court puts the boundary in the middle of the main channel or the main navigable channel.

But this is not always true. Along the Ohio River the boundary is the low water line of the northern shore (*Handly's Lessee v. Anthony* 1820). Along the Red River between Texas and Oklahoma, the boundary is the southern shore (*Oklahoma v. Texas* 1922), and the west side of the Chattahoochee River is Georgia's boundary (*Alabama v. Georgia* 1859). Louisiana claimed land to the western shore of the Sabine River. All four of these boundary disputes are a result of grants or cessions in which it was specifically stated where the boundary was to be placed.

In general, the same principles of accretion and avulsion apply to boundaries as to bed ownership. Boundaries are established based on the conditions that existed at statehood. The boundary will move with slow changes but not rapid ones. This is sometimes difficult to prove since the change could have occurred before an area was settled. Almost all the United States Supreme Court cases have recognized these principles. However, two recent decisions may have modified the common law.

The Sabine Lake and River form part of the boundary between Texas and Louisiana. An 1819 treaty with Spain established the international boundary as the west bank. This was accepted by its successors, Mexico and Texas. When Louisiana was admitted as a state in 1812, the description of the state boundary as well as the 1803 treaty with France, put the boundary as the middle of the river. The later treaty with Spain left the ownership of the western half of the river in doubt. When Texas joined the Union the boundary was described as the west bank. In 1848 both states petitioned Congress for the land in question. Congress granted Texas the power to extend its boundaries to include ". . . one half of Sabine Pass, one half of Sabine Lake, also one half of Sabine River . . ." (9 Stat. 245).

Louisiana claimed all of the land to the western shore in a later dispute (*Texas v. Louisiana* 1973). It argued that the treaty with Spain automatically extended the state boundaries to the western bank since the state boundaries were the same as those of the United States. It argued that if the boundary was the west bank at statehood, it must be still. Although Congress has the power to establish boundaries, Louisiana argued that Congress cannot change the boundaries without a state's consent (*Washington v. Oregon* 1908).

The Supreme Court disagreed with this approach. It decided the boundary should be the geographic center of the river. The concept of 'thalweg' was ignored in interpreting 'one half.' The court said the intent of Congress must control and in this instance 'one half' means one half the distance between the banks, not the middle of the main channel of navigation. The court also held the western half of the channel had been part of Louisiana before 1812. Also, since the grant to Texas did not include islands, some federal islands may exist. Any formed after 1848 belong to Texas but those formed between 1812 and 1848 may be federal.

There are several strange things about this case. It seems to ignore the prohibition on changing state boundaries without a state's consent. When Louisiana was created, the traditional boundary would have been the middle of the channel. How could Congress change that in 1848 without state consent? How are 'middle' and 'one half' different if 'middle' has been interpreted to mean the middle of the deepest channel; why not 'one half?'

Another recent case seems to have abandoned traditional principles as well. In *Ohio v. Kentucky* (1980) the United States Supreme Court refused to follow the principle of accretion. In this case Ohio had sued to determine the 1792 north shore low water mark. The "northerly edge" of the Ohio River had been recognized as the state boundary when Ohio became a state, but what did that mean? If Ohio could convince the court to use the low water line that existed in 1792, it would gain jurisdiction over an area above the waterline that had since been inundated as a result of a small dam. In its decision the Court said the doctrine of accretion did not apply to this case because of the historic situation that exists. The decision remains unclear.

The circumstances of these two cases may be slightly unusual, and the departure from an accepted and well established body of law will probably not be continued.

6

Policy Issues and Future Research

It has not been impossible to explain fully all the legal issues related to water. For example, numerous articles have been written on public access to water, with many of them covering only a single state (Frank 1983; Knuth 1978; Livingston 1980; Note 1968; Note 1978; Templar 1980b; Waite 1958a, 1962, 1965; Weston 1976). Thus the general principles described in this brief summary may not apply to a specific situation or state.

Because water law is complex, generalizations can be misleading if readers assume law is always clear and definitive. I hope this book has demonstrated that law is often ambiguous if not conflicting. If everyone agreed what the law was in a specific situation, there would be less need for lawyers to go to court. Even if agreement occurs at one point in time, concepts like 'navigation' change. There are many aspects of water law that were discussed only briefly — if at all. There is much room for geographic research in these areas, as well as in those discussed more fully.

The adjudication of Texas water rights has been discussed by one geographer (Templar 1980c), but there is a need for research in other states and for comparative studies. What are the differences in procedures used in these states? Which systems are most efficient and most equitable? Many of the available water resources in the West exist because of federal reclamation projects. What does this mean for the allocation of state water rights? In many places water quality is the most important issue. Do current laws address this problem adequately? Should federal or state laws establish water policy? Who should control atmospheric water? Is there a need for a federal ground water policy (Aiken 1982)?

Public access to water for recreation and the use of water for instream purposes was discussed briefly. A policy seems to be evolving which opens up more water to public use and allows instream uses in the West. These laws are based on the public trust doctrine or some other legal theory (Watson 1982). Is this good policy? If public rights exist, should they be regulated to prevent over-use? Courts will not control these public activities in most circumstances. How can state or local governments fulfill this role? If public rights are created where they were thought not to exist before, what happens to the expectation of the property owners who thought they had private rights? Should they be compensated for the loss they suffered (Futterman and Nixon 1983)?

There are several recent Supreme Court decisions on compacts between states (*Texas v. New Mexico* 1983; *Colorado v. New Mexico* 1982) as well as several ongoing disputes on compacts. Other recent cases on ground water (*Sporhase v. Nebraska* 1982) and on anadromous fish (*Idaho v. Oregon* 1983) show the tensions that exist between states when these shared resources become allocation issues. What is or should be the role of the federal government and the courts in resolving disputes between states (Hostyk 1982; Ladd 1981)? Is a national policy needed or should problems be resolved as they occur (Shea 1982)?

In the eastern states traditional issues were more likely to concern water quality than water quantity. Nonconsumptive uses were disputed more because there was an abundance of water. In some areas of the East this is no longer true. Does the current system need to be modified (Baram and Miyares 1982; Davis 1982a, 1982b; Putt 1981)? If it does, in what way? Since the old riparian law does not allow interbasin transfers, does this create inequitable water shortages? What are the environmental and social consequences if interbasin transfers are allowed (Abrams 1983)?

In riparian rights states, no permanent secure right is obtained in the use of water. A subsequent use may begin which interferes with an established right. Is the courts' balancing test used to determine reasonableness unfair or inefficient? Will investors refuse to spend money on water projects because their investment is insecure? Are these real problems in the riparian system, or is the current law adequate to handle these problems (Tarlock 1983b)? If change is needed, what kind should it be? Should vested property rights as exist in the West be created, or should there be administrative flexibility in allocating rights in time of shortage? Since vested water rights primarily protect consumptive uses, is this needed in the East (Ausness 1983)?

In the western states where the appropriation doctrine controls water rights, the range of problems has a different emphasis. Nonconsumptive instream uses are becoming more important to the public. Should water users be allowed to dry up a stream? Should minimum stream flows be required? What are the environmental consequences if they are not? The appropriation system may waste water because the priority system prevails and traditional technology is acceptable (Pring and Tomb 1979; Shupe 1982). Is priority in time rather than priority based on the use of water the fairest way to allocate rights? Should conservation be mandatory? Is flexible planning possible with vested water rights? Since water rights are attached to specific property, how can they be transferred (Johnson et al. 1981)? Should transfers be allowed to interfere with existing rights?

In many states there have been suggestions to change the current water law. In the East, permit systems now exist in some states, but few are comprehensive. Is a comprehensive water law needed? Can it be established with imperfect knowledge? Should laws be passed in anticipation of a problem or does "water law develop best when it responds to a perceived problem" (Tarlock 1983b:541) rather than a hypothetical future situation?

Any time a change in water policy is suggested, a variety of political groups become involved. In the West one of the quickest ways to create excitement is to recommend a change in the appropriation system. Those with vested property rights feel threatened and new potential users see opportunity. A good example of the politics of water can be seen in the struggle to pass a ground water code in Arizona (Kyl 1982). Who are the lobbyists in these situations? Where is the power to make changes? Would a change in the law be more likely through legislative action or initiative?

River banks and channels continually change. This creates continuing controversies over control of both the bed and the upland areas (Note 1983). Is the current law the best policy to resolve this? Is there a role geographers can play as expert witnesses? Is more research needed before this can occur?

If these numerous issues are put in terms of the model presented in Chapter 2, the following general questions arise. How is water being used? Does it have an influence on the landscape? How is water distributed and how does this affect other places? What influence does law have on the three questions above? Do these laws and their results reflect the goals of society? What are the political and legal processes that can be used to change the law if it fails to reflect policy goals? Are there procedures that help or hinder these processes? Are there conflicts that need to be resolved between different levels of government because of overlapping jurisdiction? Are there resource allocation problems that occur because boundaries may arbitrarily allocate a shared resource? What additional problems does this create in resource management, if the boundary is not stationary?

There are many possibilities for future research on water related issues, primarily because of the increase in the number of uses for water and the finite quantity that is easily available. Geographers have a role in this research, and many are involved. Future water policy will be influenced by the linkage between law, geography, and water resources.

Cases Cited

Adams v. Grigsby, 152 So. 2d 619 (La. 1963).

Adams v. Portage Irrigation Reservoir Power Co., 72 P. 2d 648 (Ut. 1937).

Alabama v. Georgia, 64 U.S. 505 (1859).

Albuquerque v. Reynolds, 379 P. 2d 73 (N.M. 1963).

Arizona v. California, 373 U.S. 546 (1963).

Arizona v. California, 103 S. Ct. 1382 (1983).

Arizona v. San Carlos Apache Tribe of Arizona, 103 S. Ct. 3201 (1983).

Arkansas v. Tennessee, 246 U.S. 158 (1918).

Arkansas v. Tennessee, 310 U.S. 563 (1940).

Arnold v. Mundy, 6 N.J.L. 1 (1821).

Attorney General v. Philpot (1631), cited in *Attorney General v. Richards*, 145 Eng.
    Rep. 980 (Ex. 1795).

Baker v. Ore-Ida Foods, Inc., 513 P. 2d 627 (Id. 1973).

Barney v. Keokuk, 94 U.S. 324 (1876).

Boehmer v. Big Rock Irr. Dist., 48 P. 908 (Cal. 1897).

Bohn v. Albertson, 238 P. 2d 128 (Cal. 1951).

Bonelli Cattle Co. v. Arizona, 414 U.S. 313 (1973); 495 P. 2d 1312 (Ariz. 1972); 489 P.
    2d 699 (Ariz. 1971).

Bott v. Com'n of Natural Resources, Etc., 327 N.W. 2d 838 (Mich. 1982).

Brewer-Elliot Oil & Gas Co. v. United States, 260 U.S. 77 (1922).

Brockman v. Grand Canal Co., 76 P. 602 (Ariz. 1904).

Brown v. Board of Education, 347 U.S. 483 (1954).

Cartwright v. Public Service Co. of New Mexico, 343 P. 2d 654 (N.M. 1958).

C.F.&I. Steel Corp. v. Purgatory R. Water Cons. Dist., 515 P. 2d 456 (Colo. 1973).

City and County of Denver v. Northern Colorado Water Cons. Dist., 276 P. 2d 992
    (Colo. 1954).

City of Albuquerque v. Reynolds, 379 P. 2d 73 (N.M. 1962).

City of Altus v. Carr, 255 F. Supp. 828 (W.D. Tex. 1966) aff'd mem. 385 U.S. 35 (1966).

City of Corpus Christi v. City of Pleasanton, 276 S.W. 2d 798 (Tex. 1955).

City of Los Angeles v. Baldwin, 53 Cal. 469 (1879).

City of Los Angeles v. City of Glendale, 142 P. 2d 289 (Cal. 1943).

City of Los Angeles v. City of San Fernando, 537 P. 2d 1250 (Cal. 1975).

City of Los Angeles v. Hunter, 105 P. 755 (Cal. 1909).

City of Los Angeles v. Los Angeles Farming and Milling Co., 93 P. 869 (Cal. 1908).

City of Los Angeles v. Pomoroy, 57 P. 585 (Cal. 1899).

City of San Diego v. Cuyamaca Water Co., 287 P. 475 (Cal. 1930).

City of Tacoma v. Taxpayers of Tacoma, 357 U.S. 320 (1958); 371 P. 2d 938 (Wa.
    1962); 307 P. 2d 567 (Wa. 1957); 262 P. 2d 214 (Wa. 1953).

Collin v. Gerhardt, 211 N.W. 115 (Mich. 1926).

Colorado v. New Mexico, 103 S. Ct. 2558 (1983).

Colorado River Water Cons. Dist. v. Twin Lakes Res. and Canal Co., 506 P. 2d 1226 (Colo. 1973).

Conant v. Jordan, 77 Atl. 938 (Me. 1910).

County of Trinity v. Andrus, 438 F. Supp. 1368 (E.D. Cal. 1977).

Crawford v. Hathaway, 93 N.W. 781 (Neb. 1903).

Day v. Armstrong, 362 P. 2d 137 (Wyo. 1961).

Diana Shooting Club v. Husting, 145 N.W. 816 (Wis. 1914).

Elk-Rifle Water Co. v. Templeton, 484 P. 2d 211 (Colo. 1971).

El Paso v. Reynolds, 563 F. Supp. 379 (D.N.M. 1983).

Empire Water and Power Co. v. Cascade Town Co., 205 F. 123 (8th Cir. 1913).

England v. Ally Ong Hing, 459 P. 2d 498 (Ariz. 1969).

Ex parte Boyer, 109 U.S. 629 (1884).

Featherman v. Hennessy, 113 P. 751 (Mont. 1911).

Federal Power Commission v. Oregon, 349 U.S. 435 (1955).

Feliz v. City of Los Angeles, 58 Cal. 73 (1881).

Four Counties Water Users Ass'n v. Colorado River Water Cons. Dist., 414 P. 2d 469 (Colo. 1966).

Fundingsland v. Colorado Ground Water Commission, 468 P. 2d 835 (Colo. 1970).

Gibbons v. Ogden, 22 U.S. 1 (1924).

Hall v. Kuiper, 510 P. 2d 329 (Colo. 1973).

Handly's Lessee v. Anthony, 18 U.S. 374 (1820).

Hardin v. Jordan, 140 U.S. 371 (1891).

Hardy v. Beaver County Irrigation Co., 234 P. 2d 524 (Ut. 1924).

Hardy Salt Co. v. Southern Pac. Trans. Co., 501 F. 2d 1156 (10th Cir. 1974).

Hartman v. Tresise, 84 P. 685 (Colo. 1905).

Hawkins v. Alaska Freight Lines Inc., 410 P. 2d 992 (Aka. 1966).

Hoefs v. Short, 273 S.W. 785 (Tex. 1925).

Hood & Sons v. Dumond, 336 U.S. 525 (1949).

Howard v. Ingersoll, 54 U.S. 381 (1851).

Hudson Water Co. v. McCarter, 209 U.S. 349 (1908).

Hunter v. United States, 388 F. 2d 148 (9th Cir. 1967).

Hutchinson v. Watson Slough Ditch Co., 101 P. 1059 (Id. 1909).

Idaho v. Oregon, 103 S. Ct. 2817 (1983).

In re Water Rights in Silvies River, 237 P. 322 (Ore. 1925).

Iowa v. Illinois, 147 U.S. 1 (1893).

Irwin v. Phillips, 5 Cal. 140 (1855).

Ivanhoe Irrigation Dist. v. McCracken, 357 U.S. 275 (1958).

Johnson v. Seifert, 100 N.W. 2d 689 (Minn. 1960).

Jones v. Conn, 64 P. 855 (Ore. 1901).

Kaiser Aetna v. United States, 444 U.S. 164 (1979).

Kelly ex rel. MacMullen v. Hallden, 214 N.W. 2d 856 (Mich. 1974).

Knight v. U.S. Land Association, 142 U.S. 161 (1891).

Lamprey v. Metcalf, 53 N.W. 1139 (Minn. 1893).

LeMunyon v. Gallitin Valley Ry. Co., 199 P. 915 (Mont. 1921).

Le Roy v. Trinity House, 82 Eng. Rep. 986 (K.B. 1662).

Lord Fitzwalters Case, 86 Eng. Rep. 766 (K.B. 1674).

Lundberg v. Notre Dame, 282 N.W. 70 (Wis. 1938).

Luscher v. Reynolds, 56 P. 2d 1158 (Ore. 1936).

Lux v. Haggin, 10 P. 674 (Cal. 1886).

Manry v. Robison, 56 S.W. 2d 438 (Tex. 1932).

Maricopa County, etc. v. Southwest Cotton Co., 4 P. 2d 369 (Ariz. 1931).

Martin v. Waddell, 41 U.S. 234 (1842).

Mason v. Hoyle, 14 Atl. 786 (Conn. 1888).

Mathers v. Texaco, 421 P. 2d 771 (N.M. 1966).

McNaughton v. Eaton, 242 P. 2d 570 (Ut. 1952).

Medano Ditch Co. v. Adams, 68 P. 431 (Colo. 1902).

Minnesota v. Wisconsin, 252 U.S. 273 (1919).

Moore v. Sanborne, 2 Mich. 520 (1853).

Murphy v. Ryan, 2 Ir. R.C.L. 143 (1868).

Nebraska v. Iowa, 143 U.S. 359 (1892).

Nekoosa Edwards Paper Co. v. Railroad Commission 228, N.W. 144 (Wis. 1929) aff'd
    per curium 283 U.S. 787 (1931).

Nevada v. United States, 103 S. Ct. 2906 (1983).

New Jersey v. Delaware, 291 U.S. 361 (1934).

New Mexico Products Co. v. New Mexico Power Co., 177 P. 2d 634 (N.M. 1937).

Ohio v. Kentucky, 444 U.S. 335 (1980).

Oklahoma ex. rel. Phillips v. Guy F. Atkinson Co., 313 U.S. 508 (1941).

Oklahoma v. Texas, 258 U.S. 574 (1922).

Oklahoma Water Res. Bd. v. Central Okl. Master Conservancy Dist., 464 P. 2d 748
    (Okla. 1969).

Oregon ex. rel. State Land Board v. Corvallis Sand and Gravel Co., 429 U.S. 363
    (1977) 582 P. 2d 1352 (Ore. 1978); 538 P. 2d 70 (Ore. 1975); 536 P. 2d 517 (Ore.
    1975); 526 P. 2d 469 (Ore. 1974); 439 P. 2d 575 (Ore. 1968).

Packer v. Bird, 137 U.S. 661 (1891).

Parsons v. Ft. Morgan Res. & Irr. Co., 136 P. 1024 (Colo. 1913).

Pecos County Water Control and Improvement Dist. v. Williams, 271 S.W. 2d 503 (Tex.
    1954).

Pennsylvania Natural Weather Ass'n v. Blue Ridge Weather Modification Ass'n, 44
    Pa. D.&C. 749 (1968).

People v. Emmert, 597 P. 2d 1025 (Colo. 1979).

People v. Mack, 97 Cal. Rptr. 448 (1971).

Pike v. Bruce Church, Inc., 397 U.S. 137 (1970).

Pollard's Lessee v. Hagen, 44 U.S. 212 (1845).

Rex v. Smith, 99 Eng. Rep. 283 (K.B. 1780).

Reynolds v. Miranda, 493 P. 2d 409 (N.M. 1972).

Reynolds v. Sims, 377 U.S. 533 (1964).

Richards Irr. Co. v. Westview Irr. Co., 80 P. 2d 458 (Ut. 1938).

Riordan v. Westwood, 203 P. 2d 922 (Ut. 1949).

Roberts v. Taylor, 181 N.W. 622 (N.D. 1921).

United States v. Utah, 283 U.S. 64 (1931).

Utah v. United States, 403 U.S. 9 (1971); 425 U.S. 948 (1976); 1976 *Utah Law Re.*
245 Master's Report.

Vernon Irrigation Co. v. City of Los Angeles, 39 P. 762 (Cal. 1895).

Warren v. Matthews, 91 Eng. Rep. 312 (K.B. 1703).

Washington v. Oregon, 211 U.S. 127 (1908).

Watkins v. Dorris, 64 P. 840 (1901).

Wilbour v. Gallagher, 462 P. 2d 232 (Wa. 1969).

Wilson v. Omaha Indian Tribe, 442 U.S. 653 (1979).

Winters v. United States, 207 U.S. 564 (1908).

Wisconsin v. Michigan, 295 U.S. 455 (1935).

Bibliography

Abrams, R.H. 1980. "Government Expansion of Recreational Water Use Opportunities," *Oregon Law Review* 59:159-199.

Abrams, R.H. 1983. "Interbasin Transfer in a Riparian Jurisdiction," *William and Mary Law Review* 24:591-623.

Ackerman, E. 1956. "Questions for Designers of Future Water Policy," *Journal of Farm Economics* 38:971-80.

Ackerman, E. et al. 1965. *The Science of Geography*. Washington, DC: National Academy of Sciences — National Research Council.

Ahmad, N. 1953. "The Indo-Pakistan Boundary Disputes Tribunal, 1949-1950," *Geographical Review* 43:329-337.

Aiken, J.D. 1980. "Nebraska Groundwater Law and Administration," *Nebraska Law Review* 59:917-1000.

Aiken, J.D. 1982. "Groundwater Mining Law and Policy," *University of Colorado Law Review* 53:505-528.

Alchian, A. and H. Demsetz. 1973. "The Property Rights Paradigm," *Journal of Economic History* 33:16-27.

Alexander, L. 1953. "Recent Changes in the Benelux-German Boundary," *Geographical Review* 43:69-76.

Alexander, L. (editor). 1967. *The Law of the Sea: Offshore Boundaries and Zones*. Columbus: Ohio State University Press.

Alexander, L. 1968. "Geography and the Law of the Sea," *Annals, Association of American Geographers* 58:177-197.

Alexander, L. 1979. "The Seventh Session of the Third United Nations Conference on the Law of the Sea," *Geographical Review* 69:349-350.

Anderson, T. and P. Hill. 1975. "The Evolution of Property Rights: A Study of the American West," *Journal of Law and Economics* 18:163-179.

Anderson, T. (editor). 1983. *Water Rights, Scarce Resource Allocation, Bureaucracy, and the Environment*. San Francisco: Pacific Institute for Public Policy Research.

Archer, J. 1980. "Political Geography (Progress Report)," *Progress in Human Geography* 4:255-264.

Ausness, R. 1977. "Water Use Permits in a Riparian State: Problems and Proposals," *Kentucky Law Journal* 66:191-265.

Ausness, R. 1983. "Water Rights Legislation in the East: A Program for Reform," *William and Mary Law Review* 24:547-590.

Bagley, E. 1961. "Water Rights Law and Public Policies Relating to Ground Water Mining in the Southwestern States," *Journal of Law and Economics* 4:144-174.

Baram, M. and J.R. Miyares. 1982. "In Order to Have Water: Legal, Economic and Institutional Barriers to Water Reuse in Northern New England," *New England Law Review* 17:741-776.

Barlow, I.M. 1981. *Spatial Dimensions of Urban Government*. Chichester, UK: Wiley (Research Studies Press).

Beard, D. 1975. "United States Environmental Legislation and Energy Resource Review," *Geographical Review* 65:229-244.

Beck, R. 1967. "The Wandering Missouri River: A Study in Accretion Law," *Nor Dakota Law Review* 43:429-466.

Bennett, J. 1948a. "Some Uncertainties in the Law of Water Rights," *Southern California Law Review* 21:344-356.

Bennett, J. 1948b. "Some Fundamentals of Legal Interests in Water Supplies," *Southern California Law Review* 22:1-15.

Bergman, E. 1975. *Modern Political Geography.* Dubuque, IA: Wm. Brown.

Beuscher, J.H. 1961. "Appropriation Water Law Elements in Riparian Doctrine States," *Buffalo Law Review* 10:448-458.

Blackman, J. 1982. "Public Land Law Reform-Reflections from Western Water Law," *Brigham Young University Law Review* 1982:1-59.

Boggs, S.W. 1937. "Problems of Water Boundary Definition — Median Lines and International Boundaries Through Territorial Waters," *Geographical Review* 27:445-456.

Boggs, S.W. 1951. "National Claims in Adjacent Seas," *Geographical Review* 41:185-209.

Botkin, D. and E. Keller. 1982. *Environmental Studies.* Columbus, OH: Charles E. Merrill.

Bowman, I. 1923. "An American Boundary Dispute — Decisions of the Supreme Court of the United States with Respect to the Texas-Oklahoma Boundary," *Geographical Review* 13:161-189.

Brunn, S. 1974. *Geography and Politics in America.* New York: Harper & Row.

Burghardt, A. 1973. "The Bases of Territorial Claims," *Geographical Review* 63:225-244.

Burnett, A. and P. Taylor (editors). 1981. *Political Studies From Spatial Perspectives.* New York: John Wiley & Sons.

Capone, D. and A. Ryan. 1973. "The Regional Sea: A Theoretical Division of the Gulf of Mexico and the Caribbean Sea," *Transactions of the Miami Geographical Society* 3:1-9.

Cashman, V. (editor). Dates vary. *State Court Organization Profile Series,* Williamsburg, VA: National Center for State Courts.

Changnon, S. 1977. "The Technical and Economic Aspects of Weather Modification: A Background for Lawyers," *Southern Illinois Law Journal* 1977:326-358.

Chorley, R. (editor). 1969. *Water, Earth, and Man.* London: Methuen and Co. Ltd.

Christopher, A. 1971. "Colonial Land Policy in Natal," *Annals,* Association of American Geographers 61:560-575.

Clark, R. 1960. "The Pueblo Rights Doctrine in New Mexico," *New Mexico Historic Review* 35:265-283.

Clark, R. 1977. "The Role of State Legislation in Groundwater Management," *Creighton Law Review* 10:469-487.

Cockburn, C. 1977. *The Local State.* London: Pluto.

Cohen, S. and L. Rosenthal. 1971. "A Geographic Model for Political Systems Analysis," *Geographical Review* 61:5-31.

Comment. 1976. "Subsidence: Settling Down Within the Laws of Accretion, Reliction, Erosion, and Submergence," *Baylor Law Review* 28:319-337.

Comment. 1977a. "Land Accretion and Avulsion: the Battle of Blackbird Bend," *Nebraska Law Review* 56:814-835.

Comment. 1977b. "Log Flotation as Evidence of Title Navigability," *Oregon Law Review* 56:107-123.

Comment. 1979. "Need for a Uniform Public-Private Boundary: Application of the High Water Boundary to Inland Navigable Lakes," *University of California Davis Law Review* 12:125-164.

_____ment. 1981a. "After the Flood, Who Owns the Bed of the River? State Ownership Overwhelmed by the Avulsion Rule," *Oregon Law Review* 60:273-286.

_____ment. 1981b. "Do State Water Anti-Exportation Statutes Violate the Commerce Clause? or Will New Mexico's Embargo Law Hold Water?" *Natural Resources Journal* 21:617-630.

_____ommentary. 1977. "The Public Trust Doctrine and Ownership of Florida's Navigable Lakes," *University of Florida Law Review* 29:730-751.

Committee on Atmospheric Sciences, National Research Council. 1973. *Weather and Climate Modification: Problems and Progress.* Washington DC: National Academy of Sciences.

Corker, C. 1971. *Groundwater Law, Management, and Administration.* Washington, DC: National Water Commission Legal Study 6.

Cox, K. 1968. "Suburbia and Voting Behavior in the London Metropolitan Area," *Annals,* Association of American Geographers 58:111-127.

Cox, K. 1973. *Conflict, Power and Politics in the City: A Geographic View.* New York: McGraw Hill.

Cox, K. 1979. *Location and Public Problems. A Political Geography of the Contemporary World.* Chicago: Maaronfa.

Cox, K. and F. Nartowicz. 1980. "Jurisdictional Fragmentation in the American Metropolis: Alternative Perspectives," *International Journal of Urban and Regional Research* 4:196-211.

Cox, K. and R. Johnston (editors). 1982. *Conflict, Politics and the Urban Scene.* London: Longman.

Cushing, S. 1920. "The Boundaries of the New England States," *Annals,* Association of American Geographers 10:17-40.

Davis, P. 1978. "State Ownership of Inland Waters — A Summary and Reexamination," *Nebraska Law Review* 57:665-703.

Davis, P. 1982a. "The Riparian Right of Streamflow Protection in the Eastern States," *Arkansas Law Review* 36:47-80.

Davis, P. 1982b. "Eastern Water Diversion Permit Statutes: Precedents for Missouri," *Missouri Law Review* 47:429-470.

Davis, R.J. 1974. "Weather Modification Law Developments," *Oklahoma Law Review* 27:409-439.

Davis, R.J. 1977. "The Total State Legal Regime," in B. Farhar (editor), *Hail Suppression, Society and Environment.* Boulder, CO: Institute of Behavioral Science.

Davis, R.J. 1978. "Weather Modification, Stream Flow Augmentation, and the Law," *Rocky Mountain Mineral Law Institute* 24:833-863.

David, R.J. and L. Grant (editors). 1978. *Weather Modification — Technology and Law.* Boulder, CO: Westview.

Deasy, G. 1942. "Spanish Territorial Boundary Changes in Northwest Africa," *Geographical Review* 32:303-306.

deBlij, H. 1973. *Systematic Political Geography.* New York: John Wiley and Sons.

deBlij, H. and D. Capone. 1969. "Wildlife Conservation Areas in East Africa: An Application of Field Theory in Political Geography," *The Southeastern Geographer* 9:93:107.

Dennis, A. 1980. *Weather Modification by Cloud Seeding.* New York: Academic Press.

Dewsnup, R. 1971. *Legal Protection of Instream Water Values.* Washington, DC: National Water Commission Legal Study 8-A.

Dye, T. 1964. "Urban Political Integration: Conditions Associated with Annexation in American Cities," *Midwest Journal of Political Science* 8:430-446.

Easterly, E. 1977. "Global Patterns of Legal Systems: Notes Toward a New Geojurisprudence," *Geographical Review* 67:209-220.

Easton, D. 1953. *The Political System.* New York: Knopf.

Easton, D. 1965. *A Framework for Political Analysis.* Englewood Cliffs, NJ: Prentice Hall.

Ericsson, R. 1979. "The Navigation Servitude and Reserved Indian Property: Does the Rule of No Compensation Apply to Indian Interests in Navigable Waters?" *Utah Law Review* 1979:57-76.

Evans, A. 1951. "Riparian Rights in Artificial Lakes and Streams," *Missouri Law Review* 16:93-117.

Farhar, B. and J. Mews. 1977. "Governing Weather Modification," in B. Farhar (editor), *Hail Suppression, Society and Environment.* Boulder, CO: Institute of Behavioral Science.

Farnham, W. 1972. "The Permissible Extent of Riparian Land," *Land and Water Law Review* 7:31-61.

Fielding, G. 1964. "The Los Angeles Milkshed: A Study of the Political Factor in Agriculture," *Geographical Review* 54:1-12.

Fielding, G. 1965. "The Role of Government in New Zealand Wheat Growing," *Annals, Association of American Geographers* 55:87-97.

Fischer, W. 1975. "Weather Modification and the Right of Capture," *Natural Resources Journal* 8:639-658.

Fitzsimmons, A. 1980. "Environmental Quality as a Theme in Federal Legislation," *Geographical Review* 70:314-327.

Folk-Williams, J. 1982. *What Indian Water Means to the West.* Santa Fe: Western Network.

Frank, R. 1983. "Forever Free: Navigability, Inland Waterways, and Expanding Public Interest," *University of California Davis Law Review* 16:579-629.

Freeze, R.A. and J. Cherry. 1979. *Groundwater.* Englewood Cliffs, NJ: Prentice Hall.

Fuller, H. 1976. "Landownership and the Lindsey Landscape," *Annals, Association of American Geographers* 66:14-24.

Futterman, M. and C.B. Nixon. 1983. "The Public Trust After 'Lyon' and 'Fogerty': Private Interests and Public Expectations — A New Balance," *University of California Davis Law Review* 16:631-660.

Gibson, M. 1976. "Indian Claims in the Beds of Oklahoma Watercourses," *American Indian Law Review* 4:83-90.

Glassner, M.I. 1970. "The Rio Lauca: Dispute over an International River," *Geographical Review* 60:192-207.

Gleason, V. 1977. "*Los Angeles v. San Fernando:* Groundwater Management in the Grand Tradition," *Hastings Constitutional Law Quarterly* 4:703-714.

Gottman, J. 1952. "The Political Partitioning of Our World: An Attempt at Analysis," *World Politics* 4:512-519.

Gottman, J. (editor). 1980. *Centre and Periphery: Spatial Variation in Politics.* Beverly Hills, CA: Sage.

Grant, D. 1981. "Reasonable Groundwater Pumping Levels Under the Appropriation Doctrine: The Law and Underlying Economic Goals," *Natural Resources Law Journal* 21:1-36.

Greenland, D. 1983. *Guidelines for Modern Resource Management,* Columbus, OH: Charles E. Merrill.

Griswold, E. 1939. "Hunting Boundaries with Car and Camera in the Northeastern United States," *Geographical Review* 29:353-382.

Gudgin, G. and P.J. Taylor. 1979. *Seats, Votes and the Spatial Organization of Elections.* London: Pion.

Hall, P. 1974. "The New Political Geography," *Transactions, Institute of British Geographers* 63:48-52.

Hanks, E.M. 1968. "The Law of Water in New Jersey," *Rutgers Law Review* 22:621-715.

Harrison, D. and G. Sandstrom. 1971. "The Groundwater-Surface Water Conflict and Recent Colorado Water Legislation," *University of Colorado Law Review* 43:1-48.

Hartshorne, R. 1933. "Geographic and Political Boundaries in Upper Silesia," *Annals,* Association of American Geographers 23:195:228.

Hartshorne, R. 1936. "Suggestions on the Terminology of Political Boundaries," *Annals,* Association of American Geographers 26:56-57.

Hartshorne, R. 1950. "A Functional Approach in Political Geography," *Annals,* Association of American Geographers 40:95-130.

Higdon, P. and T. Thompson. 1980. "The 1980 Arizona Groundwater Management Code," *Arizona State Law Journal* 1980:621-671.

Hill, J. 1965. "El Chamizal: A Century Old Boundary Dispute," *Geographical Review* 55:510-522.

Hodgson, R. and R. Smith. 1979. "Boundary Issues Created by Extended National Marine Jurisdiction," *Geographical Review* 69:423-433.

Hoffman, A. 1981a. *Vision or Villany, Origins of the Owens Valley — Los Angeles Water Controversy.* College Station: Texas A&M Press.

Hoffman, G.W. (editor). 1981b. *Federalism and Regional Development.* Austin: University of Texas Press.

Hornbeck, D. 1979. "The Patenting of California's Private Land Claims, 1851-1885," *Geographical Review* 69:434-448.

Hostyk, A. 1982. "Who Controls the Water? The Emerging Balance Among Federal, State, and Indian Jurisdictional Claims and Its Impact on Energy Development in the Upper Colorado and Upper Missouri River Basins," *Tulsa Law Journal* 18:1-78.

House, J. 1959. "The Franco-Italian Boundary in the Alpes Maritimes," *Transactions,* Institute of British Geographers 26:107-131.

Howe, C. et al. 1982. "The Performance of Appropriative Water Rights Systems in the Western United States During Drought," *Natural Resources Journal* 22:378-389.

Hutchins, W. 1960. "Pueblo Water Rights in the West," *Texas Law Review* 38:748-762.

Jackson, W.A.D. 1958. "Whither Political Geography?" *Annals,* Association of American Geographers 48:178-183.

Johannson, B.N. 1977. "An Examination of the Law of Water Boundaries and Accretions in Manitoba," *Manitoba Law Journal* 8:403-416.

Johnson, D. 1917. "The Role of Political Boundaries," *Geographical Review* 4:208-213.

Johnson, J. 1980. "The 1980 Arizona Groundwater Management Act and Trends in Western Groundwater Administration and Management: A Mineral Industry Perspective," *Rocky Mountain Mineral Law Institute* 26:1031-1103.

Johnson, R.N. et al. 1981. "The Definition of a Surface Water Right and Transferability," *Journal of Law and Economics* 24:273-288.

Johnson, R.W. 1971. *Law of Interbasin Transfers.* Washington, DC: Water Commission Legal Study 7.

Johnson, R.W. and R. Austen. 1967. "Recreation Rights and Titles to Beds on Western Lakes and Streams," *Natural Resources Journal* 7:1-52.

Johnston, R.J. 1979. *Political, Electoral and Spatial Systems.* London: Oxford University Press.

Johnston, R.J. 1980a. "Electoral Geography and Political Geography," *Australian Geographical Studies* 11:37-50.

Johnston, R.J. 1980b. "Political Geography without Politics," *Progress in Human Geography* 4:439-446.

Johnston, R.J. and D.J. Rossiter. 1981. An Approach to the Delimitation of Planning Regions," *Applied Geography* 1:55-69.

Jones, S. 1945. *Boundary Making: A Handbook for Statesmen, Treaty Editors and Boundary Commissioners.* Washington DC: Carnegie Endowment for International Peace.

Jones, S. 1954. "A Unified Field Theory of Political Geography," *Annals,* Association of American Geographers 44:111-123.

Jones, S. 1959. "Boundary Concepts in the Setting of Place and Time," *Annals,* Association of American Geographers 49:241-255.

Kahrl, W. 1982. *Water and Power: The Conflict over Los Angeles' Water Supply in the Owens Valley.* Berkeley: University of California Press.

Kasperson, R. 1969. "Political Behavior and the Decision-Making Process in the Allocation of Water Resources Between Recreational and Municipal Use," *Natural Resources Journal* 9:176-211.

Kasperson, R. and M. Breitbart. 1973. *Participation, Decentralization and Advocacy Planning.* Washington, DC: Association of American Geographers, Resource Paper 25.

Kasperson, R. and J. Minghi (editors). 1969. *The Structure of Political Geography.* Chicago: Aldine.

Kazman, R. 1972. *Modern Hydrology.* New York: Harper & Row.

King, P. 1978. "Exclusionary Zoning and Open Housing: A Brief Judicial History," *Geographical Review* 68:459-469.

Kinney, C.S. 1912. *Irrigation and Water Rights.* San Francisco: Bender-Moss Co.

Knuth, R.L. 1978. "Bases for the Legal Establishment of a Public Right of Recreation in Utah's 'Nonnavigable' Waters," *Journal of Contemporary Law* 5:95-110.

Kristof, L. 1959. "The Nature of Frontiers and Boundaries," *Annals,* Association of American Geographers 49:269-282.

Kyl, J. 1982. "The 1980 Arizona Groundwater Management Act: From Inception to Current Constitutional Challenge," *University of Colorado Law Review* 53:471-503.

Ladd, D. 1981. "Federal and Interstate Conflicts in Montana Water Law: Support for a State Water Plan," *Montana Law Review* 42:267-314.

Large, D. 1957. "Cotton in the San Joaquin Valley: A Study of Government in Agriculture," *Geographical Review* 47:365-380.

Leighty, L. 1970. "The Source and Scope of Public and Private Rights in Navigable Waters," *Land and Water Law Review* 5:391-440.

Leighty, L. 1971. "Public Rights in Navigable State Waters — Some Statutory Approaches," *Land and Water Law Review* 6:459-490.

Leopold, L. 1974. *Water, A Primer.* San Francisco: W.H. Freeman and Co.

Lewis, P. 1965. "The Impact of Negro Migration on the Electoral Geography of Flint, Michigan, 1932-1962: A Cartographic Analysis," *Annals,* Association of American Geographers 55:1-25.

Ley, D. and J. Mercer. 1980. "Location Conflict and the Politics of Consumption," *Economic Geography* 56:89-109.

Linsley, R. *et al.* 1975. *Hydrology for Engineers.* New York: McGraw-Hill Book Co.

Livingston, M. 1980. "Public Recreation Rights in Illinois Rivers and Streams," *DePaul Law Review* 29:353-381.

Loeffler, M.J. 1970. "Australian-American Interbasin Water Transfer," *Annals,* Association of American Geographers 60:493-516.

Logan, W.S. 1968. "The Changing Landscape Significance of the Victoria-South Australia Boundary," *Annals,* Association of American Geographers 58:128-154.

MacDonald, J. and J. Beuscher. 1973. *Water Rights.* Madison, WI: American Printing and Pub. Inc.

MacGrady, G. 1975. "The Navigable Concept in the Civil and Common Law: Historic Development, Current Importance, and Some Doctrines that Don't Hold Water," *Florida State University Law Review* 3:513-615.

MacGrath, P. 1927. "The Labrador Boundary Decision," *Geographical Review* 17:643-660.

Maloney, F. 1978. "The Ordinary High Water Mark: Attempts at Settling an Unsettled Boundary Line," *Land and Water Law Review* 13:465-499.

Maloney, F. and R. Ausness. 1975. "The Use and Legal Significance of the Mean High Water Line on Coastal Boundary Mapping," *North Carolina Law Review* 53:185-273.

Martin, L. 1930. "The Michigan-Wisconsin Boundary Case in the Supreme Court of the United States, 1923-26," *Annals,* Association of American Geographers 20: 105-163.

Marts, M. and W. R. D. Sewell. 1960. "Conflict Between Fish and Power Resources in the Pacific Northwest," *Annals,* Association of American Geographers 50:42-50.

Massam, B. 1972. *The Spatial Structure of Administrative Systems.* Washington DC: Association of American Geographers, Resource Paper 12.

Mayer, H. 1964. "Politics and Land Use: The Indiana Shoreline of Lake Michigan," *Annals,* Association of American Geographers, 54:508-523.

McGowen, J. 1956. "The Development of Political Institutions on the Public Domain," *Wyoming Law Journal* 11:1-15.

McKinley, C. 1952. *Uncle Sam in the Pacific Northwest.* Berkely: University of California Press.

Meyers, C. 1971. *A Historical and Functional Analysis of the Appropriation System.* National Water Commission Legal Study No. 1.

Meyers, C. and A. D. Tarlock. 1980. *Water Resources Management.* Mineola, NY: The Foundation Press, Inc.

Michener, J. 1974. *Centennial.* New York: Random House.

Minghi, J. 1961. "The Conflict of Salmon Fishing Policies in the North Pacific," reprinted from *Pacific Viewpoint* in Kasperson and Minghi 1969.

Minghi, J. 1963. "Boundary Studies in Political Geography," *Annals,* Association of American Geographers 53:407-428.

Minghi, J. 1981. "Recent Developments in Political Geographical Research in North America," 33-42 in Burnett and Taylor 1981.

Minghi, J. and D. Rumley. 1978. "Toward a Geography of Campaigning: Some Evidence from a Provincial Election in Vancouver, B.C.," *The Canadian Geographer* 22:145-162.

Mitchell, B. 1976. "Politics, Fish and International Resource Management: The British-Icelandic Cod War," *Geographical Review* 66:127-138.

Mitchell, B. 1979. *Geography and Resource Analysis.* New York: Longman.

Mitchell, J. 1978. "The Expert Witness: A Geographer's Perspective on Environmental Litigation," *Geographical Review* 68:209-214.

Morrill, R. L. 1973. "Ideal and Reality in Reapportionment," *Annals,* Association of American Geographers 63:463-477.

Morrill, R. L. 1976. "Redistricting Revisited," *Annals,* Association of American Geographers 66:548-556.

Morrill, R. L. 1981. *Political Redistricting and Geographic Theory,* Washington, DC: Association of American Geographers, Resource Publication.

Muir, R. 1975. *Modern Political Geography.* London: MacMillan.

Muir, R. 1976. "Political Geography: Dead Duck or Phoenix?" *Area* 8:195-200.

Muir, R. and R. Paddison. 1981. *Politics, Geography and Behavior.* London: Methuen.

National Water Commission. 1973. *Water Policies for the Future.* Washington, D
National Water Commission.

Nelson, H. 1952. "The Vernon Area, California — A Study of the Political Factor ir Urban Geography," *Annals,* Association of American Geographers 42:177-191.

Norris, R. and L. L. Haring. 1980. *Political Geography.* Columbus, OH: Charles Merrill.

Note. 1968. "Fishing and Recreation Rights in Iowa Lakes and Streams," *Iowa Law Review* 53:1322-1346.

Note. 1972. "Artificial Additions to Riparian Land: Extending the Doctrine of Accretion," *Arizona Law Review* 14:315-343.

Note. 1978. "Water and Water Courses — Recreational Rights — A Determination of the Public Status of West Virginia Streams," *West Virginia Law Review* 80:356-368.

Note. 1979. "Indian Rights to Lands Underlying Navigable Waters: State Jurisdiction Under the Equal Footing Doctrine vs. Tribal Sovereignty," *North Dakota Law Review* 55:453-474.

Note. 1980. "Subsidence: An Emerging Area of the Law," *Arizona Law Review* 22:891-917.

Note. 1981a. "Navigable Water Not Always Subject to Free Public Access," *Natural Resources Journal* 21:161-168.

Note. 1981b. "Public Use — the Effect of Property Law as a Limitation on Federal Navigational Servitude," *Florida State University Law Review* 89:209-219.

Note. 1983. "Real Property: The Stability of Riparian Land Titles and the Wild and Unruly Cimarron River," *Oklahoma Law Review* 36:229-243.

O'Loughlin, J. 1980. "The Election of Black Mayors, 1977," *Annals,* Association of American Geographers 70:353-370.

Ostrom, V. 1953. *Water and Politics: A Study of Water Policy and Administration in the Development of Los Angeles.* Los Angeles: The Haynes Foundation.

Pattison, W. 1957. *The Beginnings of the American Rectangular Land Survey System 1784-1800.* Chicago: The University of Chicago Department of Geography Research Paper 50.

Pearcy, G. E. 1959. "Geographical Aspects of the Law of the Sea," *Annals,* Association of American Geographers 49:1-23.

Pearcy, G. E. 1973. *A Thirty-Eight State U.S.A.* Fullerton: Plycon.

Pierce, J. 1967. "Legal Aspects of Weather Modification Snowpack Augmentation in Wyoming," *Land and Water Law Review* 2:273-319.

Plater, Z. 1974. "The Taking Issue in a Natural Setting: Floodlines and the Police Power," *Texas Law Review* 52:201-256.

Platt, R. H. 1976. *Land Use Control: Interface of Law and Geography.* Washington, DC: Association of American Geographers, Resource Paper 75/1.

Pounds, N. J. G. 1959. "A Free and Secure Access to the Sea," *Annals,* Association of American Geographers 49:256-268.

Pounds, N. J. G. 1972. *Political Geography.* 2d ed. New York: McGraw Hill Book Co.

Prescott, J. R. V. 1959a. "Nigeria's Regional Boundary Problems," *Geographical Review* 49:485-505.

Prescott, J. R. V. 1959b. "The Function and Methods of Electoral Geography," *Annals,* Association of American Geographers 49:296-304.

Prescott, J. R. V. 1972. *Political Geography.* London: Methuen.

Prescott, J. R. V. 1978. *Boundaries and Frontiers.* Totowa, NJ: Rowman and Littlefield.

Pring, G. and K. Tomb. 1979. "License to Waste: Legal Barriers to Conservation and Efficient Use of Water in the West," *Rocky Mountain Mineral Law Institute* Paper 25, 1-67.

:de, P. 1976. "The Residential-Landscape Conservation Zone as an Example of Applied Geography," *Geographical Review* 66:200-208.

:utt, L.O. 1981. "An Analysis and Evaluation of Water Rights in Alabama in Perspective with Other States in the South Atlantic and Gulf Region," *Cumberland Law Review* 12:47-98.

Quinn, F. 1968. "Water Transfers — Must the American West be Won Again?" *Geographical Review* 58:108-132.

Radosevich, G. E. et al. 1976. *Evolution and Administration of Colorado Water Law: 1876-1976.* Ft. Collins: Water Resource Publications.

Recent Developments. 1981. "Determining the Parameters of the Navigation Servitude Doctrine," *Vanderbuilt Law Review* 34:461-480.

Reed, S. 1979. "Use It or Lose It — Surface Water Rights in Idaho," *Idaho Law Review* 15:569-590.

Rice, J. 1978. "The Effect of Land Alienation on Settlement," *Annals,* Association of American Geographers 68:61-72.

Roalfe, W. 1965. *How to Find the Law.* 6th ed. St. Paul: West Pub. Co.

Roberts, M. C. and K. W. Rummage. 1965. "The Spatial Variation in Urban Left-Wing Voting in England and Wales in 1951," *Annals,* Association of American Geographers 55:161-178.

Robinson, K.W. 1962. "Political Influence in Australian Geography," reprinted from *Pacific Viewpoint* in Kasperson and Minghi 1969.

Rodda, J. (editor). 1976. *Facets of Hydrology.* New York: John Wiley and Sons.

Sack, R.D. 1972. "Geography, Geometry, and Explanation," *Annals,* Association of American Geographers 62:61-78.

Sandars, T.C. 1970. *The Institutes of Justinian with English Introduction, Translation and Notes.* Westport, CT: Greenwood Press.

Sauer, C.O. 1918. "Geography and the Gerrymander," *American Political Science Review* 12:403-426.

Sax, J. 1981. "Liberating the Public Trust from Its Historic Shackles," *University of California Davis Law Review* 14:185-194.

Sewell, W.R.D. 1966. "The Columbia River Treaty: Some Lessons and Implications," *Canadian Geographer* 10:145-156.

Shea, T. 1982. "Coordination and Consensus in Water Resource Management," *Pacific Law Journal* 13:975-1002.

Shupe, S. 1982. "Waste in Western Water Law: A Blueprint for Change," *Oregon Law Review* 61:483-522.

Smith, R. 1981. "The Maritime Boundaries of the United States," *Geographical Review,* 71:395-410.

Soja, E.W. 1971. *The Political Organization of Space.* Washington, DC: Association of American Geographers Resource Paper 8.

Sommers, L. and O. Gade. 1971. "The Spatial Impact of Government Decisions on Postwar Economic Change in North Norway," *Annals,* Association of American Geographers 61:522-536.

Spykman, N.J. 1942. "Frontiers, Security and International Organization," *Geographical Review* 32:436-447.

Stingham, R. 1966. *Magna Carta — Fountainhead of Freedom.* Rochester: Acqueduct Books.

Stone, A. 1978. *Selected Aspects of Montana Water Law.* Missoula: Mountain Press.

Sutton, I. 1976. "Sovereign States and the Changing Definition of the Indian Reservation," *Geographical Review* 66:281-295.

Tarlock, A.D. 1978. "Appropriation for Instream Flow Maintenance: A Progress Report on 'New' Public Western Water Rights," *Utah Law Review* 1978:211-247.

Tarlock, A.D. 1983a. "So It's Not 'Ours' — Why Can't We Still Keep It? A First Look at *Sporhase v. Nebraska*," *Land and Water Law Review* 18:137-174.

Tarlock, A.D. 1983b. "Introduction," *William and Mary Law Review* 24:535-545.

Taylor, P. 1978. "Political Geography," *Progress in Human Geography* 2:153-162.

Taylor, P. 1982. "Editorial Essay: Political Geography — Research Agenda for the 1980s," *Political Geography Quarterly* 1:1-17.

Taylor, P. and R. Johnston. 1979. *Geography of Elections*. London: Penguin.

Templar, O.W. 1973. "Water Law and the Hydrologic Cycle, A Texas Example," *Water Resources Bulletin* 9:273-283.

Templar, O.W. 1978. Texas Surface Water Law: the Legacy of the Past and Its Impact on Water Resource Management," *Journal of Historical Geography* 4:11-20.

Templar, O.W. 1980a. "Conjunctive Management of Water Resources in the Context of Texas Water Law," *Water Resources Bulletin* 16:305-311.

Templar, O.W. 1980b. "Problems of Public Access to Water in Texas Lakes and Streams," *Water Resources Bulletin* 16:668-675.

Templar, O.W. 1980c. "The Evolution of Texas Water Law and the Impact of Adjudication," Paper presented at the 16th American Water Resources Association Conference, Minneapolis, Minnesota.

Thomas, B. 1949. "Boundaries and Internal Problems of Idaho," *Geographical Review* 39:99-109.

Thomas, B. 1952. "The California-Nevada Boundary," *Annals, Association of American Geographers* 42:51-68.

Thomas, J.A.C. 1975. *The Institutes of Justinian: Text, Translation and Commentary*. Oxford: North Holland.

Thorton, C. and R. Koepke. 1981. "Federal Legislation, Clean Air, and Local Industry," *Geographical Review* 71:324-339.

Todd, D.K. 1980. *Groundwater Hydrology*. New York: John Wiley and Son.

Trelease, F.J. 1954. "Coordination of Riparian and Appropriative Rights to the Use of Water," *Texas Law Review* 33:24-69.

Trelease, F.J. 1961. "Federal Limitations on State Water Law," *Buffalo Law Review* 10:399-426.

Trelease, F.J. 1971. *Federal-State Relations in Water Law*. Washington, DC: National Water Commission Legal Study 5.

Trelease, F.J. 1978. "Federal-State Problems in Packaging Water Rights," in *Water Acquisition for Mineral Development*. Boulder, CO: Rocky Mountain Mineral Law Institute.

Trelease, F.J. 1979. *Water Law*. St. Paul: West Pub. Co.

Trelease, F.J. and Wright Water Engineers Inc. 1982. *A Water Protection Strategy for Montana: Missouri River Basin*. Helena: Montana Department of Natural Resources and Conservation.

Tuan, Y.F. 1968. *The Hydrologic Cycle and the Wisdom of God*. Toronto: University of Toronto Press.

Ullman, E.L. 1951. "Rivers as Regional Bonds: The Columbia-Snake Example," *Geographical Review* 41:210-225.

Waite, G.G. 1958a. "Public Rights to Use and Have Access to Navigable Waters," *Wisconsin Law Review* 958:335-375.

Waite, G.G. 1958b. "The Dilemma of Water Recreation and a Suggested Solution — Their Relation to the Northwest Ordinance, The State Constitution, and the Trust Doctrine," *Wisconsin Law Review* 1958:542-609.

Waite, G.G. 1962. "Public Rights in Indiana Waters," *Indiana Law Review* 37:467-488.

Waite, G.G. 1965. "Public Rights in Maine Waters," *Maine Law Review* 17:161-204.

Walker, R. and M. Heiman, 1981. "Quiet Revolution for Whom?" *Annals, Association of American Geographers* 71:67-83.

Walston, R. 1982. "The Public Trust Doctrine in the Water Rights Context: The Wrong Environmental Remedy," *Santa Clara Law Review* 22:63-93.

Ware, E. 1905. *Roman Water Law — Translated from the Pandects of Justinian.* St. Paul: West Pub. Co.

Water Information News Service. 1983.

Wegman, E. and D. DePriest (editors). 1980. *Statistical Analysis of Weather Modification Experiments.* New York: Macel Dekker Inc.

Weston, R.T. 1976. "Public Rights in Pennsylvania Waters," *Temple Law Quarterly* 49:515-557.

White, G.F. 1969. *Strategies of American Water Management.* Ann Arbor: University of Michigan Press.

Whittlesey, D. 1935. "The Impress of Effective Central Authority upon the Landscape," *Annals,* Association of American Geographers 25:85-97.

Whittlesey, D. 1939. *The Earth and the State: A Study in Political Geography.* New York: H. Holt & Co.

Wiel, S. 1919. "Waters: American Law and French Authority," *Harvard Law Review* 33:133-167.

Wolfe, J. and A. Burghardt. 1978. "The Neighborhood Effect in a Local Election," *Canadian Geographer* 22:298-305.

Wolman, M.G. 1967. "A Cycle of Sedimentation and Erosion in Urban River Channels," *Geografiska Annaler* 49:385-395.

Wright, C.A. 1976. *Handbook of the Law of Federal Courts.* 3rd ed. St. Paul: West Pub. Co.